HYDRO

A Beginner's Guide to Building Your
Own Hydroponic Garden

By Tom Gordon

this book has been derived from various sources. Please consult a licensed professional before attempting any techniques outlined in this book.

By reading this document, the reader agrees that under no circumstances is the author responsible for any losses, direct or indirect, which are incurred as a result of the use of information contained within this document, including, but not limited to, — errors, omissions, or inaccuracies.

Table of Contents

INTRODUCTION

When we think of gardening, what we often see in our heads is a man or a woman on all fours crouched over a plot of dirt. They dig a hole, place in a seed or even a whole plant which they have bought, close it up and there you go. Or maybe we think of gardening in line with farming and we picture the same thing, only this time there isn't someone crouched down but a series of mechanical inventions that do all that busy work for them. We almost certainly don't think of an indoor setup, as that is more in line with hanging plants and decorative greens than it is with the concept of gardening. This would suggest that our main identifier which separates gardening from owning a few plants is the dirt itself, the soil which is part of Mother Earth. But the facts are quite different.

There are many different ways of gardening. The classic flowerbed in the front yard is just one of them. Here we'll be looking at another of them: Hydroponics. To say hydroponics is a new fad in the gardening world would discredit its history which reaches all the way back to the hanging gardens of Babylon and the Aztecs' floating gardens. There are even Egyptian hieroglyphs which describe a form of hydroponic. More recently, hydroponics was even given a place within NASA's space program. Clearly, this is not a new fad. But commercial growers and scientists are coming around to the method, leading to more hydroponic setups being used and more research looking into the advantages of hydroponics.

So, what makes hydroponic gardening different than traditional gardening? As the name implies (hydro) water plays a key role. The hydroponic garden actually doesn't make use of soil. Instead, hydroponic gardens make use of nutrient-based solutions through the circulation of water. So, a hydroponic garden tosses out the soil and instead uses an inert grow medium like clay pellets, vermiculite, perlite or one of several others that will pop up throughout this book. What this does is let the roots of the plant directly touch the nutrient solution, get more oxygen as they're not buried in the ground, and together these both promote growth.

The growth that this promotes can be quite astounding. A hydroponic setup, if managed properly, can actually see your plants maturing up to 25% faster than in typical soil gardening. Not only that but those plants that grow 25% faster might also yield up to 30% more as well! This is because the plants don't need to work as hard to get nutrients in a hydroponic setup as they would in a more traditional one. Basically, with the roots getting everything they need to provide the plant with nutrients, the plant can focus on growing its top part rather than having to grow out its roots for sustenance.

But there are even more benefits to using a hydroponic setup than just expedient plant development. Despite the fact that hydro is in the name, hydroponic gardens actually use up less water than traditional soil-based gardens do. This is because the hydroponic system is an enclosed system. This means that there is less soil runoff, evaporation or wastewater in a hydroponic setup. Therefore, a hydroponic garden, when properly set up and maintained, will produce bigger plants at a faster rate with less environmental strain. It seems win-win-win, all around.

However, there are some slight disadvantages to hydroponic gardens over traditional soil-based gardens. The biggest and most obvious of these disadvantages is that a hydroponic garden will cost more to set up than a soil garden, regardless of size. With a soil garden, all you have to do is dig a hole, put in the plant or seed and then water it from time to time. This doesn't mean that you will have a healthy and well-functioning garden but it is pretty easy to get going. A hydroponic garden requires time and money to set up, especially if you've never set one up before. Plus, if you don't manage your hydroponic setup then it isn't very likely that it will keep those plants alive. Maintenance is super important here, that's why there's a whole chapter devoted to it later on. There are many different kinds of hydroponic gardens we can set up and some actually have more risks than others. For example, a setup that uses a pump (such as an ebb & flow system) can see that pump clog if not cared for properly and a clogged pump could see all your plants dead as result.

It should be noted that we are focused on hydroponic gardening which, despite the similarity in name, is not the same as aquaponic gardening. Aquaponic gardening is, in fact, a mixture of hydroponics with the growing and raising of fish. Basically, aquaponics is a hydroponic garden setup in which fish are introduced into the system. These fish create waste in the water which helps to give nutrients to the plants. The vegetables in the aquaponic garden, in return, clean the water for the fish. In this way, the aquaponic garden provides for both the fish that are being raised and the plants that are being grown. Aquaponic gardening is a great way of growing and raising food with an eye to sustainability. However, aquaponics gardening is beyond the scope of this specific book.

In this tome we will first explore the different types of hydroponic gardens we can set up. These will range from drip systems to ebb and flow systems, from aeroponics to wicking systems. We'll explore the advantages and disadvantages that they offer so that you have the knowledge you need to choose the type of system that works best for you. From there we will look into how these systems are built. While we won't be building every single kind of system that exists, we'll look at the general equipment that we need and explore the specifics of the most popular styles.

After we have our systems built, we'll talk about the operation cycle of hydroponic gardens. This means we'll explore how we set up our grow material, get seeds planted and discuss the different issues related to the lighting and trimming of our plants. Once we understand how to operate these systems, we'll take some time to examine the various plants that work best for hydroponic growth. We will also shed light on nutrition to figure out what exactly we mean when we use that word and what nutrients we feed into our systems.

With an understanding of the operation and nutrition of our hydroponic gardens, we will be able to move into a discussion on maintenance. This is one of the key areas that we need to grasp if we want to find success with our hydroponic gardens. Without proper maintenance, we can't expect to grow anything properly when we're fighting against clogs and bad pH levels. We'll move from maintenance into pests, which require another form of maintenance themselves. Thankfully, as we'll see, pests aren't nearly as common in a hydroponic setup as they are in traditional gardens. Finally, we will explore mistakes and myths that commonly pop up in regards to starting and maintaining a hydroponic garden.

While these gardens do take more time to set up than the traditional, the knowledge in this book will give you a leg up in starting your own. But the benefits of hydroponic gardening speak for themselves: bigger plants in less time. Who wouldn't want that?

CHAPTER ONE

DIFFERENT TYPES OF HYDROPONIC GARDENS

If we want to become hydroponic gardeners, the first thing we need to do is understand what options are available to us. This way we can choose a method that has advantages and disadvantages that are properly in line with what we are looking for. This means, for example, if we don't want to risk clogs, we could avoid using methods that involve pumps. However, if we live in an area where we have a hard time controlling the amount of light in our environment, we might find ourselves looking to a system that uses a pump rather than one of the simpler ones like a deep-water culture in which light regulation is also important.

Each of these systems offers unique advantages and disadvantages from which we can choose. But this does not mean that one particular system is better than another. Like most things in life, the choice of which hydroponic system to use should be based on your schedule, needs and abilities. For this reason, I won't be extolling the virtues of any one particular system. Instead, we will look at the most popular systems around to see what their benefits are and what their disadvantages are. This way, you will have the knowledge necessary to choose the type that is right for you.

Hydroponic system

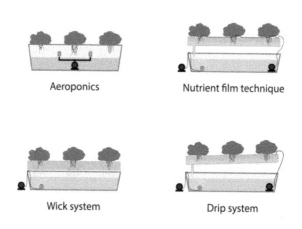

Aeroponics

Nutrient film technique

Wick system

Drip system

Drip System

This system is one of the most popular hydroponic setups but it was actually invented for outdoor gardens in Israel. At its most simplified, the drip system uses a pump to keep a drip of nutrient-rich water feeding our plants. The slow drip, rather than the typical spraying of water we see in gardens, allows for less water to be used.

Typically, a drip system is designed with two key parts. The first is the reservoir of nutrient-rich water that will feed the plants. Above this rests the grow tray in which our plants are potted. A pump is set up in the water and is connected up into the grow tray. From there, each of the plants will be given their own drip line. This means if you are growing four plants in your tray, you would use four drip lines. Sixteen plants, sixteen drip lines. However, because we want to give the growing medium, that substance you use to replace soil (and which we'll be looking at more in chapter three), time to breathe so as not to drown the plants, these drips will use a timer system. The growing medium will slowly release the water back down into the reservoir, creating a closed system.

A drip system offers us great control over the amount of water and nutrients that our plants are getting. With this system we are able to control the drip both by quantity and by length. This means if we use too much water in our drip, we can dial it back; or, if our drip is going too long or too short, we can adjust the timers that we are using to experiment until we find the length that's just right. One of the cool things about the drip system is that while it may take a while to set up and get right in the early period, once we have everything in place and know our volumes, the system doesn't require as much overall maintenance (depending on the particular setup) as other methods will. Plus, the materials needed to create a drip system aren't as costly as some of the others.

However, a drip system still uses a pump and a clogged pump can see our gardens decimated in merely a few hours. Of course, this depends on the size of the system. While the drip system is great for large-scale grow operations, it might be too complex for smaller operations. Some drip systems use what is called a non-recovery system which means that the water is not circulated back into the reservoir. These particular systems require less maintenance than systems which do feedback into the reservoir but in doing so they create more waste. This means that regardless of the system we use, we either will require more maintenance or create more waste.

A drip system works well for a variety of herbs and plants ranging from lettuce, onions, and peas to radishes, cucumbers, strawberries and pumpkins. It turns out that these systems actually are fantastic for larger plants. They also work best when making use of a growing medium in which water drains slowly like peat moss or coconut coir.

So, if you are looking to grow larger plants, the drip system is a great choice. Drip systems do require a bit of maintenance and they can be slow to set up at first but once they get going, they offer a high level of control over the growing process that any gardener would love.

Deep Water Culture

Considered the easiest of the hydroponic systems, a deep-water culture uses a reservoir system that the roots of the plants are suspended into. Basically, the plants sit above and instead of dripping water, they just reach down to take the water they want. This makes the system quite easy to set up.

A deep-water culture gets its name from the use of a deep reservoir and from how deep the roots go into the water. Other systems, such as the nutrient film technique, expose the roots of the plants to the air so that they can absorb plenty of oxygen. With this system we set up a grow tray above our reservoir, making sure that the material we use stops light getting through the system to prevent algae from growing inside and messing up the system. From there, the roots are suspended in the water and the water itself is kept oxygenated through the use of an air pump. This is done to keep the roots from drowning in the water.

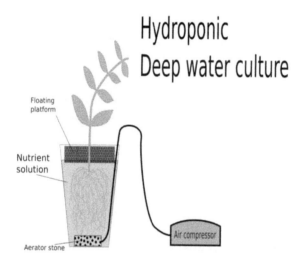

That's pretty much it. It wasn't a joke to say this is among the easiest of the hydroponic setups to get started with.

Deep water cultures are great for this simplicity but it is far from the only benefit that they offer. Because there are so few moving parts in a deep-water culture, they are rather low maintenance. There is an air pump but we don't pump water in this system and so the fear of losing our gardens to a faulty pump is unwarranted here. The easy setup and lower maintenance of these systems make them great for people first getting into hydroponic gardening and wanting to see if the approach is right for them.

However, while the deep-water culture's pump is air-based and so results in fewer blockages, they are still put at risk by power outages. Because the air pump is needed to oxygenate the water, a power outage could see your garden drown. Depending on the size of the system, it can be really tough to maintain proper pH levels in the water. A smaller system is harder to make minor changes in pH level to, as going just a little over or under can make a massive difference at smaller sizes. Finally, it can be really hard to keep a balanced water temperature in these systems as we have to be careful about the exposure of the reservoir to light.

Because of the way the system is set up, with the plants resting above the reservoir, the suitability of crops for the deep-water culture depends on several key factors. The first key is weight. If the plants we choose are too top-heavy, they can risk toppling over and breaking or even causing the weight of the setup to shift and knocking the top off. That's a disaster nobody wants to experience. The other major point is that we need to choose plants that like water. This means that plants which prefer dry growing conditions won't do very well in a deep-water culture. However, plants such as lettuce which love to soak up water will love this system.

Besides lettuce, some great choices for this system are herbs like basil and greens like kale, collard greens, chard and sorrel. Bok choy and okra also grow well in these systems and offer a variety outside of the traditional vegetables one thinks of as garden veggies.

So if you're looking to grow some water-loving plants, deep water culture is a system that is easy to set up and requires little maintenance. However, we have to be careful which plants we pick. If they are too top-heavy or prefer dry conditions, the deep-water reservoir isn't for them.

Nutrient Film Technique

With the nutrient film technique, we again use a reservoir of water but this time we are pumping it into a grow tray that has been set up at a slight angle. Doing it this way means that gravity takes care of getting the nutrient-rich water from one end of the tray to the other, where it will then drain back into the reservoir. More information about how we add nutrients to our water is covered in chapter four. Because of the design, this system is best used for plants with a smaller root system. The NFT setup is an active system.

The plants in the NFT system only have the ends of their roots touching the water, so as to keep the roots able to take in precious oxygen which helps growth. Because the system only uses a little water at a time, the plants are never drowned in the water.

Because of the way the plants are positioned, it is very easy to check the roots for disease in the NFT system. The use of a reservoir of water that feeds back into itself reduces the overall waste of water and the design of the system makes it easy to scale the project up or down depending on the size needed. Plus, unlike deep water cultures, it can be fairly easy to get the pH levels right using an NFT setup.

However, the NFT also relies on a pump and so the risk of pump failure and the decimation of your crop is still a possibility that one has to look out for. Because of the way the roots are slotted into the system, they can block up the flow of water. This is why plants with a large root system like carrots aren't a good fit for the NFT system.

Because the roots are not actually in a growing medium like the other systems we looked at, this means that top-heavy plants don't work here either. However, leafy greens like lettuce or fruits like strawberries have found great success growing through an NFT system.

Ebb and Flow

The ebb and flow system get its name from the periodic flooding and draining of nutrient-rich water. It is also known, fittingly, as the flood and drain system. In this system, water floods into the glow tray and soaks the roots of the plants. Then the water drains back down into the reservoir. Flood, drain. Flood, drain. Over and over again, hence the name.

In order to get the system to work properly, we need to set up a pump to flood the grow tray. We set this pump up on a timer rather than let it constantly flood the grow tray and drown the plants. An overflow tube is set up in the grow tray so that the water drains back down into the reservoir. Depending on how we set it up, we might even include an air pump to make sure that the roots are getting the oxygen that they need.

The nice thing about the ebb and flow system is that it doesn't cost a lot to get started, as the materials aren't particularly hard to get a hold of. This system makes sure our plants are getting enough nutrients without drowning due to the easy to build structure. Once the system is set up, the hardest part of running it is out of the way. The ebb and flow system is able to run by itself once set up but you should still do maintenance to ensure everything is working properly.

Again, this system uses a pump, which means it can break and broken pumps are notorious for killing off entire gardens. If the structure fails to drain properly, the plants risk drowning and the pH levels in a broken system can be harmful to the plants. This is important to know because this system is prone to breakdowns and so we have to understand which areas a breakdown affects most.

One of the coolest things about the ebb and flow system is that it can be set up to allow just about any kind of plant or vegetable. Not so much the plants that prefer a dry system but size is not a concern here the way that it was in the nutrient film technique setup. Because of how easy it is to build the structure; we can alter it to fit the needs of our plants rather easily.

Wicking

Out of all of the systems we have and will look at, wicking is the easiest. It is so easy, in fact, that it is often recommended as an entry point to hydroponic gardening. Wicking is a passive system with very few parts, there are no water pumps in a wicked system.

In this system, we once again fill a reservoir with water and keep it beneath a grow tray. This time however, we don't use tubing to get the water to the plants but rather we set up a wicking material like rope. This wicking material is placed into the water and threaded up into the grow tray. Our grow tray is filled with a growing medium that is good at absorbing and keeping water because this system works very slowly. Water travels the length of the wick to slowly feed the plants.

This system is great for its simplicity and can serve as an easy way to start getting into hydroponic gardening. It is also an inexpensive system, making it that much easier for the novice grower to invest in. Because there is no pump to break down, this system isn't at risk for premature death the way pump-based systems are. The lack of a pump also means that this system doesn't use up electricity and it can be refreshing to those worried about the size of their power bill.

However, despite its simplicity, there are still downsides to the wicking system that we have to consider. The system is inefficient at delivering nutrients, so plants that need a lot of water and nutrients aren't a very good match. The system can also see a toxic build-up of nutrients in the growing medium if we are not careful to observe how much water is getting in and being used.

Because of the lower water levels in wicking systems, they are best used for small plants. Lettuce and the smaller of the herbs make good fits for a wicking system but water-hungry plants like tomatoes would absolutely hate a wicking system. For this reason, the wicking system doesn't offer nearly the same variety as other systems. But that lack of variety is made up for by the ease of setup, making wicking a great system for those first trying their hands at hydroponics.

Aeroponics

Saved the most complex for last. Aeroponics does away with the growing medium and instead leaves the roots of the plants exposed to more oxygen and so this system tends to see faster growth.

In this system, the roots of the plants hang down in the open air of the container in which the system is built. At the bottom of the system is our reservoir of nutrient-rich water. However, the roots don't dangle down into the water this time. Instead, we use a pump from the water to spray the plant roots with the nutrient solution. This pump is of course set up on a timer, to ensure we aren't overfeeding the plants. This makes it so that instead of the plant spending energy to grow out longer roots in search of nutrients, the nutrients come to the roots so that the plant can focus its growth elsewhere.

This system is great for producing larger plants since they don't need to focus on root growth. The lack of a growing medium also means that the roots don't need to take hold; we are bringing the nutrients directly onto them. The exposure of the roots to oxygen also helps to promote growth. This means that the aeroponic system is known for producing crops with impressive yields. This system also doesn't require a lot of space can so it can be built to be fairly mobile. Because of the lack of a growing medium, the aeroponic system is rather easy to clean.

We have to make sure to clean it because the constantly wet atmosphere of the system makes for an environment in which bacteria and fungi can thrive. The system is also very much prone to failures related to pumps and loss of power, which we've seen can be a major killer of our hydroponic gardens. The setup of an aeroponic garden also costs more than the other systems and it is the most technical of the hydroponic systems, which means the knowledge to entry is much higher as well. They also require constant supervision to protect against root diseases, fungi and to monitor pH levels and the density of the nutrient solution.

However, this system allows for bigger yields and the system can be used to grow almost any kind of plant. This means that the variety the aeroponic system offers is unparalleled compared to the other systems we have looked at.

Choosing the System That is Right for You

Like many things in life, the choice of which hydroponic system to use is a highly personal one. Each of us is after different goals with our gardens and has different skill levels when it comes to handling the technical stuff. This means that the best option available to us in order to figure out which system to use is to ask questions based around our needs and desires, such as:

What is your skill level in putting together handy projects? If low, perhaps beginning with a wicking system would be an ideal start. What kinds of plants do you want to grow? If you are looking for top-heavy and larger plants, you are going to need to use a system that can support them. If you are looking for something smaller, you'll have more options but that doesn't mean you should go small if what you are after is a bigger plant. Do you have the time to invest in one of the more maintenance-heavy setups or would a more streamlined one like wicking fit into your life and gardening goals better?

Each of the setups that we have explored in this chapter has been written about and explored in depth throughout the internet with many first-hand accounts of how they turned out. If one strikes you as intriguing, there is always more research that can be done to make sure that it is right for you. But one thing that stands out when you research these is that each one has been used successfully and has been demonstrated to have grown some amazingly healthy- and good-looking plants.

You know what you desire more than anyone else. Looking at the benefits, the plant types and the cons should give you a good idea of where to start. I suggest narrowing down to the couple that interest you most and going from there.

Chapter Summary

- There are six main systems when it comes to hydroponic gardens.

- The drip system is designed to offer a timer-based drip onto each individual plant. It gives great control over how much water and nutrients our plants get and can be used to grow an impressive variety of plants.

- The deep-water culture is one of the easiest hydroponic setups; it allows the roots of the plant to be submerged in a nutrient solution.

- The nutrient film technique uses gravity and a water pump to soak the roots of our plants while also giving them plenty of exposure to air. NFT setups don't do well with large rooted plants or overly top-heavy ones.

- The ebb and flow systems work by flooding the plants and then draining out the water. This system can work with just about any kind of plant, giving it a lot of versatility.

- Wicking is the easiest of the hydroponic systems and takes its name from how it uses a fabric wick to transport water from the reservoir into our grow tray. This system is a great starter but it doesn't offer a ton of variety in what grows best.

- Aeroponics is a hydroponic system which relies on misting the roots of the plants. It is the most technical of the systems to set up but can be the most rewarding. It also works with a wide array of plants.

- The system that works best for you is a personal choice depending on what you desire to grow and how much time and skill you have for setting up and maintaining your system.

In the next chapter, you will learn how to build your own hydroponic garden. We will look at how to set up a drip system, a wicking system and a deep-water culture. These range from beginner to intermediate in terms of difficulty setting up and so should make great entry points to those tackling hydroponic gardening for the first time.

CHAPTER TWO

HOW TO BUILD YOUR OWN SYSTEM

Now that we know the different kinds of hydroponic setups that are available to us, it is time to see how they are built. We will be looking at three of the different setups, those most suited for beginners. As we saw previously, each system has its own pros and cons. This means that the system you choose should be the one that fits your desires. However, this chapter can also help you to determine which setup is right for you based on how difficult it is to get it running.

While there are many sites and businesses out there that will sell you hydroponic kits, it can be very easy to make them ourselves. This isn't to say there is no value in store-bought kits. But before we go spending a lot of money, a DIY setup can be a great way to get a handle on the basics of setting up a hydroponic garden. Once we know what we are doing, we can then start to add on all sorts of gears and gizmos to personalize and level up our gardens.

But we have to start somewhere and DIY is a great place to kick off from.

Drip System

For this system, we're going to look at one of the easy-to-build drip systems. This one uses buckets in which to grow the plants which still receive their nutrient-rich water through a series of tubes. In order to accomplish this design, there are three key areas which we need to build: the buckets, the reservoir and the tubing. We will look at what it takes to make a single plant setup but we'll see how easy it is to adapt the system to include more.

Start with your bucket. For our purposes, we'll begin with a five-gallon bucket but you can increase or decrease the size as necessary. The first thing we do is flip the bucket upside down so that we can get at the bottom easily. We're looking to get the drain into place so that any water dripped into the system will be recycled back into the reservoir. To do this we will be using a thru-hole fitting. These little guys are used in all sorts of different fields and you can easily pick one up for a dollar or two at any hardware store.

Place the thru hole on the bottom of the bucket, thread side making contact, and trace around it. This should give you a small little circle on the bottom of your buckets. We want this circle to be closer to the edge than to the middle, as we want our bucket to be able to sit comfortably on an elevated surface. With that in place, cut out the circle you have traced and insert the thru hole into the bucket. Tighten the thru hole in place. Your bucket now has a drain installed. Take a filter of some sort, can be a furnace filter or any kind really, and cut enough out to place over the thru hole inside the bucket. This helps to keep only water draining and not our growing medium.

Now before we move onto the next step, we should paint our buckets. We can double up this task and paint our reservoirs at the same time. Use a black paint on the outside of the bucket in order to block light from entering which would lead to algae growth. With the buckets painted black, they are going to attract a lot of heat which would raise the temperature of our water and could prove to be a real pain in the long run. For this reason, it is suggested that you use a coat or two of white paint over the black paint so as to reflect the light rather than absorb it.

We're going to do a similar design when it comes to our reservoir but the key difference is the hole we cut will be in the top and not in the bottom. Having painted the reservoir black and then white, we will cut a hole in the top of it through which we can feed the cording for our pump and for the hoses. That's all that the reservoir takes.

But in order to make this work from here, we need to connect them using tubing. Connect the tube to the hose and feed it up to the bucket. You can use glue, tape, or whatever method you prefer in order to keep the tube in place to feed your plants. One effective way is to create a loop that sits inside the inside of the bucket, poke a ton of little holes in it and then connect that tube to your main tube. That way water would flow up through the main tube, connect to the inner bucket tube and it would work like a mini sprinkler system. This way makes sure that the water is spread around the bucket and not confined to a single area.

With the feeder tube in place, we then need to attach the draining tube. This is as easy as hooking our tubing up to the thru hole we inserted and running it back down into the reservoir. It is important that we keep our grow bucket elevated above the reservoir so that gravity can do its trick.

In order to make sure that we aren't drowning our plants, it's important that we get a digital timer and hook it up so that we aren't pumping water at all times. We'll want to get a timer that allows us to set many different times rather than just one time because we want our system to turn off and on several times a day rather than just once. We need to do this in order to make sure that our plants are getting the right amount of nutrients.

So that is how you set up a single bucket drip system. If you want to expand the system, it is actually very easy. Let's say that you wanted to do four buckets instead of just one. You take those buckets and you give them their thru holes and a paint job all the same. The major difference between running a single bucket setup and a four bucket setup is the tubing. Rather than running a single tube from our reservoir to our bucket, we are going to instead use T-connectors.

Take the tubing that runs out of the reservoir and connect it into a T-connector. This will give you a tube that looks like a T-corner like we see on the roads. Instead of being a single tube with one ending, you now have two tubes each with their own ending. This would allow us to use a two bucket setup. However, we choose a four bucket setup for this example. This means that we have to take each of those tubes and again run them into a T-connector. Now each side gets split into two and we have four ends, one for each of our buckets and we have quadrupled the size of our grow operation.

With all the building in place, we then just have to pack in our buckets. Some rocks at the bottom of each bucket can serve to help weigh them down but it's not absolutely needed. This is more a precaution, though it is one that is recommended. Over the rocks, you pack in your growing medium and then you get your plants in there.

And there you have it, your very own hydroponic drip system.

Wicking System

As we saw above, wicking is actually the easiest of the systems to get started with. It's also one of the easiest systems to build as it requires very little technical skill. All we need to get started is a growing tray, a reservoir and a material for wicking.

Wicking is simply the use of a wickable material going from our reservoir to our grow tray. This can be rope, felt, string; whatever material you can easily get your hands on for the wicking will work.

We will first set up our reservoir, filling it with our nutrient solution of choice, which of course depends on what we are growing (for more information on nutrient solutions, see chapter four). Again, we are going to paint the reservoir black and then cover it in a coat of white paint to prevent it from supporting algae or growing too hot. We are then going to cut or drill very small holes in the cover of the reservoir through which we will thread our wicks.

Our grow trays are going to be filled with a medium that is particularly well-suited to wicking such as perlite or coco coir. But before we fill them up, we first want to cut or drill tiny holes into the bottom of the tray as we did to the cover of the reservoir. These will be roughly the same size because they are how the wick gets the nutrients to the plants.

Ultimately, we have our wicks almost entirely submerged in the water. This doesn't necessarily mean that they are touching the bottom of the reservoir but they are certainly coming close. They are then fed up and nested in the growing tray very close to the plants. We can use more than one wick per plant depending on the plant's particular water and nutrient needs.

As far as set up, that's really it. We place our plants into the grow tray and we watch how they grow. However, there are some tips and tricks that will make a more successful wicking system. We might consider using an air pump to aerate the water so that our plants are able to get more oxygen as this will help them to grow faster. Another thing we will want to consider is keeping the grow tray closer to the reservoir with a wicking system than we would with a drip system. This is because the nutrients aren't pumped to our plants in this system but have to rely on what is called capillary action (aka, wicking). Having our wicks shorter means, they can more easily provide. The distance between our wicks and the grow tray is one way of doing this. Another is making sure that the level of the water in our reservoir is high, as this shortens the distance as well.

Again, this system isn't great for plants that require a lot of water and nutrients because the wicking of nutrients is a slow process. However, herbs and lettuce can grow great crops in a wicking system and this makes for an easy way to introduce the concepts of hydroponics to someone new to the topic. They even make great projects for getting kids into hydroponics and gardening!

Deep Water Culture

Despite the wicking system being considered the easiest of the hydroponic systems to get started gardening with, the deep-water culture is just about as easy when it comes to building. For our purposes of explanation, we will be making a single deep-water culture. This means that we will be designing one as if we were growing a single medium-size plant. This system can be adapted to fit multiple smaller plants, though if we want to go bigger, we will have to change our culture to a larger container first.

Since a deep-water culture uses deep water (it's there in the name, after all), we will be using a five-gallon bucket because of the depth that it gives us. While some people refer to any system of plants floating on the water as a deep-water system, we actually need to have ten plus inches of water for it to be considered deep. We could grow a small plant in a small culture and have it be equivalent in ratios to that of a deep water culture but it still wouldn't be proper to call it such.

The first thing that we are going to do, surprise, is paint our bucket black and then white. Slightly underneath the lid, we are also going to cut a little hole for the tubing of our air pump so that we can oxygenate the water. With these two steps out of the way, we can set our buckets to the side.

Because a deep-water culture works by having the roots of the plant soaking in the water, we need to design a setup so that our plants can bath. To do this, we can go out and buy what is called a plant basket. This is a basket that looks like your typical plant pot but instead, it has a ton of holes through the lower half. Alternatively, we can also just take a plant pot and then cut, drill or solder holes into it. This is going to be our grow tray.

We'll be filling our grow tray up with our desired growing medium and the plant that we want to raise but first, we need to integrate it into the system. To do this we will be cutting a hole in the lid of our five-gallon bucket. At this point, it is best to cut a smaller hole and make it larger as needed rather than start with a large hole. This is because it is far easier to increase the size of the hole than it is to block it back up. If we make our hole too big, our grow tray will just fall into the bucket and we will need to get another lid and try all over again. Our goal is for the lower half of the pot to fit into the hole and be held in place by the pot's rim against the bucket's lid.

Earlier, we cut a hole in our bucket just under the lid for our air pump. The reason we didn't cut it on the lid itself is that when we open our system up to check the pH levels and make sure our nutrients are all balanced, we don't want to have to fiddle around with any wires. When we open our system, we should only have to remove the lid and thus the plant pot.

Everything should now be in place. We're going to fill up the bucket with our water, bringing it up to cover three-quarters of the plant pot that is hanging down inside it. We might want to test this first with plain water so that we can then mark the desired water level on our buckets to make it easier to see going forward. Mix together your nutrient solution, fill the plant potter with your desired growing medium and add your plant or seed.

It will take a week or so for the roots of the plant to start poking out of the holes that we drilled into our pot, so it is important to make sure that the water level is high enough for our plants to get the moisture they need. As the roots begin to hang down, the water level won't matter nearly as much.

And there you have it, you just created a deep-water culture for your plants. While you can grow a medium-sized plant or a couple of small ones in this one culture, you are most likely going to want to set up a couple. But as you've seen, that shouldn't take very much time at all.

Chapter Summary

- Building a drip system requires tubing, a reservoir, a bucket and a pump. This system requires a little bit of work but is very easy to scale to the size you require.

- In order to prevent algae from growing in our reservoirs, we paint them black. In order to prevent them from absorbing too much heat, we cover the black paint with white paint.

- All we need to set up a wicking system is to drill a hole through the top of our reservoir and the bottom of our growth tray and thread through a wickable material. This makes wicking the easiest of all the systems and great for beginners.

- A deep-water culture involves setting up a deep bucket or container of water and then hanging our growing pots down into it. This easy-to-set-up system allows us to grow one medium-sized or a handful of smaller-sized plants. While not as scalable as the drip system, ease of setup makes it a great option.

In the next chapter, you will learn all about the operation cycle of hydroponic gardens. From the choice of growing medium to how we seed our plants and from lighting to trimming. While none of these steps are particularly difficult in and of themselves, we want to make sure that we have a strong grasp of each of them.

CHAPTER THREE

OPERATION CYCLE

Now that we have got a hydroponic system set up, let us take some time to look at how the operation works. This means that we will be exploring the different kinds of growing mediums available to us to see what works best for which kinds of setups. We will also explore how we seed our hydroponic gardens, how we light them and what we do when the time comes for trimming.

Growing Mediums

When it comes to what medium we use in our grow trays, there is a ton of variety available to us. This can be a little intimidating at first when you aren't sure which medium is right for you and the gardening that you are looking to do. It is important that we choose a medium that works with the plants we are planning to plant. This means that we have to take into account things like water retention and pH balance.

Before we look at the mediums themselves, a quick word on the requirements of the different systems. The way that each system is set up and works actually says a lot about what kind of growing medium works best. For example, a drip system functions best when it is using a growing medium that doesn't become too soggy. In contrast, a wick system likes a growing medium that absorbs and holds onto water and moisture with ease. While nutrient film technique systems want to avoid a growing medium that easily saturates, an ebb and flow system will want to have good drainage and a growing medium that doesn't float. Considering the mechanics of your system of choice is the first step in deciding a growing medium.

Coco Coir

An organic and inert grow medium, coco coir is made from the frayed and ground husks of coconuts. When it comes to pH, coco coir is very close to neutral. Coco coir retains water but also allows a decent amount of oxygen to get through which helps the roots. This medium is primarily used in container growing or in hydroponic systems of the passive variety such as wicking. Because it can clog up pumps and drippers, it is not a great choice for more active systems such as the ebb and flow system.

Gravel

Gravel doesn't absorb or retain moisture. Instead, gravel works to give an anchor for the roots of the plant. For this reason, gravel works best in a system which doesn't require a ton of retention such as a drip system or a nutrient film technique system. Any system that keeps the roots of the plant in constant contact with the water can make good use out of gravel.

In some setups, such as the bucket-based drip system we saw above, gravel is used as a bottom layer in the pot. This allows for better drainage as the water has passed through whatever medium made up the top layer to find gravel which doesn't retain it whatsoever. It also serves to add some weight to the bottom of your tray which can help to prevent spills from wind or other elements.

If you are using gravel, make sure to give it a proper wash before use in the system. If you want to reuse the gravel, make sure to wash it yet again. We do this to prevent salts or bacteria from getting into the hydroponic system and causing issues such as burnt roots, high levels of toxicity and the like. Jagged gravel can also damage the roots so it is best to use smooth gravel as a way of avoiding this.

Perlite

Perlite is actually an amendment to our growing mediums, which means that it is used to improve an existing medium rather than just being used on its own. You make perlite by heating up glass or quartz sand, though of course we don't have to make it ourselves but can buy it from any gardening store. Perlite helps to improve the drainage and aeration when mixed in with another growing medium such as coco coir.

Because we are using a nutrient mix and not just pure water, we have to be concerned about nutrient build-up. The nutrients in our solutions can get absorbed into the grow medium and lead to a build-up of toxicity which risks killing off our plants No gardener wants that. The extra drainage that perlite offers will help to prevent this build-up and will help in making sure that our plant's root system get the oxygen it needs to grow. Perlite comes in different grades from fine and medium through to coarse. The kind you need will be determined by the rest of your potting mix. Perlite should never take up more than a third of your mix, however, as using too much will cause it to float and floating perlite doesn't offer the benefits, we wanted it for in the first place.

Vermiculite

Vermiculite is actually a lot like perlite. It comes in three different grades, again ranging from fine and medium through to coarse. Made by expanding mica through heat, vermiculite is another soil and potting mix amendment. This means that vermiculite is mixed with another growing medium in order to get the best results.

Vermiculite sort of works like the reverse perlite. Where perlite helped with the drainage of our growing medium, vermiculite helps our growing medium to retain water. For this reason, vermiculite can often be seen mixed with perlite for use in hydroponic systems of the passive variety such as wicking systems.

Rockwool

One of the most popular of the growing mediums, Rockwool is made through the heating and spinning of certain silica-based rock into a cotton candy-like material. This creates a firm material that tends to have the ideal ratio of water to oxygen that our plants' roots love. It also is mostly pH neutral, which is always a plus.

It can be found in a bunch of different shapes and sizes with the most common being a cube shape. These cubes are awesome for starting out seeds (which we'll look at more in just a moment). These smaller cubes are often used in order to begin the growing of a plant before being transferred into another growing medium.

Because of the versatility of Rockwool, it can be used for starting plants before transferring into another medium for deep water cultures or nutrient film technique systems. It can also be used for drip systems and ebb and flow systems without the need to transfer.

Mixing Your Growing Medium

When it comes to which growing medium is the best, it depends on the job that you are looking to have it tackle. Once you have an idea of what you need, you can begin the task of mixing it all together. There are many different projects on the market that offer pre-mixed growing mediums and these can be a great way to save a little time and get what you need right out of the box.

However, some of us are a little more specific and we like to get our hands dirty in this part of the process. Mixing your own growing medium can be a great way to make sure it is 100% the way you want it to be. But this can be a little tricky if you are new to hydroponic gardening and don't know what combination of mediums is best. Part of getting into anything new, and hydroponic gardening is no different, is that you have to accept some uncomfortable moments and you have to accept that you will learn from your mistakes.

For an example of one mixture, let us look at what Upstartfarmers.com have laid out in their discussion on soilless potting. They offer a formula for a mixture that is one-part coconut coir or peat, one-part perlite or vermiculture and two parts compost. While the systems we have looked at aren't focused on compost but rather getting nutrients through our reservoir's solution, this shows us a straightforward mixture. Notice that the perlite or vermiculite does not exceed 33% (or 1/3rd) of the total mixture.

Seeding

When it comes to getting plants into our hydroponic system, we have two options available to us. We can go to the store and we can purchase a seedling which we then transplant into our system. Or we can purchase seeds and we can raise the plants ourselves. In this section, we will be looking at this second option to see how it is we can turn seeds into wonderful plants for our hydroponic gardens. But this means that we will also be exploring the first option because when our seeds are ready to be moved into our hydroponic setups, we will be transplanting them as seedlings.

There is a lot of satisfaction to be found in growing a plant out of a seed. They start out as tiny grains and yet can grow to be such big and luscious plants. It really is a wonderful feeling to know that you are the one responsible for making that come to pass. But there are benefits to growing from seed beyond just the feeling that it gives us.

When you purchase seeds, you are getting many chances at growing the plants you want. Not every seed will take but enough of them will that you can easily get a ton more plants through seeds for the same price that you would go out and get a single seedling. This makes it a cost-effective approach, as well as one that just feels really awesome. Purchasing seeds also gives you more control over what you grow, as you are not limited in options to only the seedlings that the store had available when you went looking. This means that you can be the one to choose what you grow and it could be rare and esoteric plants or just some lettuce and herbs. The choice is up to you.

If you grow the seeds directly in the hydroponic system which you are planning to use, then you don't have to worry about transplanting your greens into a new system. This can be a way to avoid causing the plants trauma or ending up with root damage.

Transplanting into the system can also be a way to introduce disease or pests into your garden and we want to avoid this whenever possible.

When we decide that we are going to start with seeds, it does cost us a little bit of money upfront because we need to create a few things for them to start to grow. However, this cost is mostly when just beginning. If you have already started with seeds before, you can expect to save some money when you come to them next. The good news is that you really don't need to go out of your way to buy super specialized equipment or materials to begin growing from seeds. All of the materials that you pick up can have uses at other steps in the process.

Assuming that you have already gone and picked out some seeds, what do you need to get them started in your hydroponic garden? The first thing we need is a grow tray. This can be one that we have set up before, or we can make one with a dome shape to it so as to create a miniature greenhouse. Don't worry if you don't have one that fits that description, this is just one way to help our seeds out. We can use whatever grow tray we have available.

We want to make sure that we position our grow tray so that it gets good light - if the plants are the type that likes lots of light. We also want to make sure that the tray gets a good amount of heat. Getting a heating pad that goes under or making sure it is kept in a warm area will help to make sure that sprouting begins to happen.

At this stage, we have two options available to us. Our grow tray can be used specifically just for these seeds, which would mean that we have to transplant them when they have grown into seedlings, or we can use a grow tray that is ultimately part of the hydroponic setup itself. Going the second route can be useful because it avoids the traumas that can happen when trying to transplant our seedlings.

After we have a tray set up, we are going to want to go out and get or make some starting plugs. These are little compact masses of solid growing medium that are used specifically for the growing of our seeds They tend to be made up of composted pine and peat or other organic matter. We can purchase them or make them, as they are basically little cubes of the material with a small hole for us to put our seeds into.

Open up your plug and drop a couple of seeds inside of it. We do a couple just in case any of the seeds don't want to take. If multiple take, we can always remove the weaker plant so that the stronger one can grow even better. After you have dropped your seeds into the hole, tear off a tiny piece of the plug and use it to block the hole. You do this to prevent your seeds from drying out or getting knocked out of the plug.

In the grow tray, you will need about an inch of nutrient solution, though you only want that inch to be at half the strength that it would normally be at. Place the seeded plugs into the tray. You can expect to start seeing some sprouts emerge within four or five days from planting. Make sure that you keep an eye on the water levels throughout this period and add more nutrient solution as the levels decrease.

That's how you grow from seed. Now, if you have set this up in your main grow tray, you don't have to worry about transplanting them later and you can just let them grow and continue watching them as you would any other plant in your garden. If you started them in a tray specifically for seeds, however, then you are going to need to transplant them into your system.

As your seedlings start to grow stronger, you can stop worrying about halving the strength of the nutrient solution and begin them on the regular strength solution mix. When you start to see the roots of the seedlings coming out of the bottom of the starter plug, this is the sign that you can now begin transplanting them. This could be anywhere from two to four weeks; it all depends on which plants you are growing.

Now that the seedlings are ready, you are going to take them and gently move them over to your hydroponic setup. To do this you are going to take the seedling and the cube together. You want to open up a spot in your garden, gently place the cube and seedling into said spot and then cover it gently with your growing medium of choice. After this is done, you will want to water the plant from the top for a few days so that it grows out its root system and naturally seeks out water and nutrients.

And that's it! Now you have grown your very own plant from seed through to seedling and all the way through transplanting and developing a root system naturally. Working with seeds this way allows us to take more control over what we grow and to make sure that we aren't introducing any problems into our garden that may be found in the seedlings available for purchase at the store.

Lighting

When it comes to lighting, there can be no substitute that makes up for the power of the sun. There is a reason that spring and summer are such beautiful, green times of the year. The sun is absolutely the most powerful lighting source available for plants.

But we're not going to be using it here, despite all that. Instead, we are going to be using artificial lighting so that we have complete control over it. Not only that, but many of us are interested in hydroponics because we don't have access to an outdoor space in which to garden. If you live in an apartment, chances are you're reading this because it offers you an option for growing your own food without having to leave home. If you can set up your hydroponic garden so that it takes advantage of natural sunlight, that's great! But if you can't, you need to look into artificial lighting and that's what we'll be exploring.

There are tons upon tons of options available for lighting. So many that it can be really overwhelming if you are new to the topic. What size light do you want? What color spectrum is it supposed to be playing within? Heck, how much light is the right amount? It can truly be daunting. But don't worry, it's a lot easier than all those choices make it out to seem.

Tackling the amount of light, we can use the sun as a basis for this. If we were growing plants outside, we can expect them to need about five hours of direct sunlight and another ten of indirect sunlight. This means five hours soaking in the sun and ten hours being outside but getting a little shade. Using this system, we can adjust our artificial lighting accordingly. Using artificial lights, we should be giving our hydroponic garden about fourteen hours of bright light and ten hours of darkness. Doing this system everyday imitates the sun's natural lighting cycle. Don't skimp on the darkness, either. You might think that more light means faster growth but plants are just like us in that they need to rest and metabolize the nutrients that they are getting.

Some plants need more light, some plants need less. You can think of the fourteen-ten system as a general. This system works well for most plants and can definitely be a successful route to take with your garden. But you should definitely be aware of the light requirements of your plants.

Some plants like short days, which means they want longer periods of darkness in which to function. With these plants, being exposed to more than twelve hours of light per day can actually cause them to not flower properly. Strawberries and cauliflower are examples of short-day plants. The short-day cycle actually works to imitate the shorter days of the spring in which these plants like to grow.

Long-day plants are those that want to get up to eighteen hours of sunlight per day. These ones are mimicking the longer day cycle that comes with the summer season. Examples of long-day plants include lettuce, potatoes, spinach and turnips. Because they like more light, you wouldn't want to mix long-day plants with short-day plants in the same growing tray. If you do, expect to pick a lighting cycle that meets in the middle of long and short needs.

There are also plants which are more neutral. These plants tend to be flexible and can work with more or less light as needed. Eggplant and corn are examples of these sorts of plants. Day-neutral plants can be mixed together with either short-day or long-day plants and grow equally well.

Because you want to mimic the sun, the best option for lighting your hydroponic garden is to get a timer. If you set up an ebb and flow system earlier, you probably have already gotten yourself a timer to make sure that you are letting your nutrient solution drain before washing over them again. We basically use the same kind of timer, only instead of being set up to a pump, we have set it up to our lights. How long you set the timer for will depend on what you are growing and their light needs as discussed above.

When it comes to the lights themselves, we need to get into a discussion on bulbs. The most popular bulb to use in hydroponics tends to be between 400-600 watts and of a kind called High-Intensity Discharge. These bulbs tend to be encased in glass (with gas and metal salts thrown into the mix) and they create light through sending electricity between two electrodes within. The gas helps the bulb to create the arc and the metal salts evaporate to make white light. They come in two types: high-pressure sodium bulbs and metal halide bulbs.

The metal halide bulb works as an all-round light that most vegetables will love. If you have to choose between metal halide or high-pressure sodium bulbs, the metal halide is the better choice. They tend to be expensive, upwards of $150 for a 400-watt bulb but they only need to be replaced every other year, though they may decrease in efficiency earlier.

High-pressure sodium bulbs are best used for the flowering stage of our plants. These are even more expensive than metal halide bulbs but they tend to last up to twice as long. However, they do also lose efficiency like the metal halide bulbs.

If we want to increase the efficiency of our bulbs, we can use a reflector hood. This is a reflective case that goes around the bulb and increases its effectiveness by bouncing the light around. This helps the light to hit our plants from different angles so that we can get a more effective spread onto our garden. It also serves to get a little more heat out of the bulbs, as the light beams are now crossing each other and make up a denser section and thus carry more heat and power.

So when it comes to lighting, if you can only get one bulb, go out and get yourself a metal halide bulb and a reflector hood. Get yourself a timer and make sure that you set it to the needs of your plants. When buying plants, you almost always will receive a tag with some information about the light requirements of the plant or the seeds. Following this and setting up an appropriate timer will make sure that your plants get all the light they need.

Trimming

The final step in the operation cycle of our hydroponic gardens is trimming. When plants are out in the wild, nature plays the role of gardener and trimmer. These plants can go many years, sometimes even their whole life, without being trimmed or pruned. Once you bring your plants indoors, either inside with a hydroponic setup or in a greenhouse, people immediately start reaching for those pruning shears. When we consider the image of gardening we have in our heads, we can see that movies and TV have told us again and again that we want to prune our plants. Characters are always doing it!

But the truth is that if we don't prune our plants properly, we actually risk hurting them. To be clear, this means that the pruning we are doing is the thing that can hurt them. Not a lack of pruning. Improper pruning causes unneeded stress on our plants and can do some serious damage to them, even going so far as to leave them vulnerable to disease or infection. This is because each time we prune our plants, what we are doing is opening up a wound. We cut off a branch, we have just torn open our plants. Where there was a hand, figuratively, there is now just a stump. If you think about the human body, you can see why this could easily go wrong. We need to give our plants' bodies the same respect we would give another human's. This means that when you go to prune, make sure that you sterilize your cutting instrument between every cut. This can be done as simply as mixing four parts water with one-part bleach and dunking your shears into the solution before each cut.

So if pruning our plants can be so harmful, what are the reasons that we choose to do it? There are actually quite a few reasons. One is that we want to control the overall size of our plants. If we are growing inside, we may prune our plants to prevent them from reaching out and getting in the way of walking areas or the television, things like that. This is the same reason that we cut tree branches when they get too close to power lines. We might also cut our plants to improve their health and the quality of their flowering. If a particular piece of the plant is dead and rotting, we need to remove that piece to promote the plant's health. We may also want to remove bits that didn't flower properly, that way the healthy flowering parts have more room to breathe and space to expand. This will also stop the plant from spending energy trying to repair damaged parts and instead it can use that energy for growing.

One reason NOT to trim your plants is to increase the overall yield. Trimming doesn't help our plants in this way. Rather than trim to increase, we should be trimming to promote better health.

When we have decided where we plan to prune, we know we need a sterilizing solution for our shears. Another way to prevent diseases during the pruning process is to pinch the ends of the plant where you have made the cut. This will help to get the ends to heal together quicker. It's kind of like stitching up a cut on your arm. You want to keep the ends together so that healing is promoted and the time it takes to heal is reduced. Because pruning the plant is so stressful and healing takes energy, you should really only prune when absolutely necessary and you shouldn't just make cuts willy nilly. It might be best to prune a little, wait for the plant to heal and then prune some more rather than do it all in one big burst.

If the reason you are pruning your plant is that it is growing too high for the area you are housing it in, consider doing what is called "topping." When we prune in this manner, what we are doing is cutting off the top of the main stem of the plant. Once we make the cut, we are going to then pinch it together as we do with any of our cuts. However, pinching the top of the main stem after a cut gets the plant to release floral hormones which will cause the plant to begin focusing on growing sideways rather than upwards. This same technique can then be applied to these lateral branches to achieve a reverse effect where it begins to grow upwards again. In this way, topping allows us to get some control over the growing patterns of our plants. Topping also leads to a weird effect where gardeners have noticed that plants which have been topped tend to produce more small fruit. Meanwhile, plants that haven't been topped tend to produce less fruit but of a large size.

If you are pruning to remove damaged and dying leaves, you should only be removing leaves that are more than half damaged. These leaves are no longer providing the plant with energy and instead are actually draining it of some in its attempts to heal them. There is a misguided idea that if a plant's leaves turn yellow, you should immediately remove them. However, turning leaves yellow is actually the plant's way of trying to tell you that something is wrong. It typically means that the plant is undergoing a lot of stress. This could mean that it isn't getting the nutrients and light it needs or maybe it is even a sign that the plant is dealing with an insect problem.

When your plant's leaves start turning yellow, you should look at what the plant is trying to tell you before you start to cut it. If you fix the problem, quite often you will see the leaves take on their healthier green color again.

So, when it comes time to start pruning your plants, make sure that you sterilize your instruments, think about how much stress you are putting on the plant and only make cuts that are absolutely necessary. We want to grow healthy and fruitful plants and this means respecting the bodies of your plants like you would respect your own.

Chapter Summary

- There are many different growing mediums available to us on the market today. We can even mix together our own if we want.

- Coco Coir retains water but allows decent oxygen to get through. However, it is prone to clogging up pumps.

- Gravel doesn't retain moisture but serves to anchor our plants. It is also good for weighing down our grow trays so they don't accidentally spill.

- Perlite is best used in addition to another growing medium and helps to offer better drainage.

- Vermiculite is the reverse perlite; we add it to another growing medium in order to help with retaining moisture.

- Rockwool offers a lot of versatility as a growing medium and is great for starting out your seeds.

- Purchasing seeds tends to be better than buying seedlings as it gives us more chances to grow plants and a better control over what plants we want to grow.

- We start our seeds out in starting plugs in a grow tray with a nutrient solution at half the strength of our regular system.

- Once the seeds begin to sprout, we transfer the seedling (starting plug and all) into our hydroponic setup.

- When it comes to lighting our hydroponic garden, we aim to recreate a light cycle similar to the sun. The plants we are growing will determine if we need more or less light hours than a typical day.

- Trimming our plants is actually a form of harming them and so we should only prune our plants when we absolutely have to.

- If we are pruning for size, we should be considering a topping method so that we can control how they grow out.

In the next chapter, you will learn all about the plants that work best in our hydroponic gardens. Not only that but we will take a look at the nutrients we are feeding them.

CHAPTER FOUR

BEST PLANTS FOR HYDROPONIC GARDENING AND NUTRITION

We know what each of the hydroponic garden setups are, how we make several of our own and what kind of operation cycle we can expect to be going through. In this chapter, we are going to take a look at the different plants that are available for us to grow. We will take a brief look at each plant to get an idea of how they best grow in our hydroponic setups. From there we will be looking at the nutrition that our plants require.

Vegetables

When it comes to vegetables, there are a ton of options available to us. We'll be looking at a handful of these but first, let's tackle some general rules of thumb.

First up are those vegetables that grow underneath the soil. These are vegetables like onions, carrots and potatoes. These plants can still be grown in a hydroponic system but they require extra work compared to those that grow above the surface like lettuce, cabbage and beans. This means that those under-the-soil plants require a little more advanced skill, and you may want to get some experience with your hydroponic system before you try to tackle them.

The other rule of thumb is that we should try to avoid crops like corn and zucchini and anything that relies on growing lots of vines. These types of plants take up a ton of space and just aren't very practical crops for hydroponic systems. Instead of focusing on a plant type that isn't practical, we can make better use of our space and systems.

Beans

There are many different types of beans from green beans to pole beans, lima beans to pinto beans. Depending on the type of bean you plant, you may want to consider adding a trellis to your setup. Beans offer a wide variety for what you can add them to and they make a great side dish to just about any meal.

When it comes to temperature, beans prefer a warm area. They also prefer a pH level of around 6.0.

If you are growing your beans from seeds, you can expect them to take between three and eight days to germinate. From there you can expect another six to eight weeks before it is time to harvest. After harvesting begins, the crop can be continued for about another three or four months.

Cucumbers

Like beans, there are a few different options when it comes to what kind of cucumber we can grow. There are thick-skinned American slicers, smooth-skinned Lebanese cucumbers, seedless European cucumbers. So a wide variety, and the best news is they all grow pretty well in a hydroponic setup. Where beans prefer a warm temperature, cucumbers prefer straight-up hot. They like to be a step beyond just warm. They also prefer a pH level between 5.5 and 6.0

It only takes between three and ten days for cucumbers to begin to germinate. They take between eight to ten weeks to get ready for harvesting. When it comes to harvesting cucumbers, make sure that the cucumbers have taken on a dark green color and that they are firm when you grasp them. Because each cucumber grows at a different rate, you can expect the harvesting to take some time as you don't want to pick them before they are ready.

Kale

Kale is a delicious and nutritious vegetable that makes a great addition to just about any meal. There are so many health benefits to kale that it is often considered a superfood. Kale actually prefers a slightly cooler temperature; it grows best in a range between cool to warm. Like cucumbers, kale prefers a 5.5 to 6.0 pH level.

Seed to germination only takes four to seven days. However, to get harvesting takes between nine and eleven weeks. It's a little bit longer to grow kale than either beans or cucumbers but you can harvest it in such a way so that it continues to grow. If you only harvest 30% of your kale when it comes time, this lets it quickly regrow. Doing this means that you can easily keep this superfood in your garden and in your diet.

Lettuce

As you have been reading through this book, I would bet it's safe to say that no plant has popped up more often in our discussion than lettuce. This is because lettuce absolutely thrives in hydroponic growing conditions, which is great since lettuce can be used to make salads, give some texture and flavor to our sandwiches and burgers and is just an all-round versatile vegetable to have in the kitchen.

Growing lettuce offers a lot of variety. While lettuce prefers a cool temperature and a pH level between 6.0 and 7.0, it works in any of the hydroponic systems which you have made. For this reason, lettuce makes a great entry plant for getting into hydroponics. Lettuce only takes a couple of days to germinate but the time to harvest depends on what kind of lettuce you decided on growing. For example, loose-leaf lettuce only takes forty-five to fifty days to get to harvest. Romaine lettuce can take up to eighty-five days.

Peppers

Like tomatoes, peppers are technically a fruit but are so tightly linked to vegetable-based dishes and crops that many people think of them as vegetables. For that reason, we'll be looking at both peppers and tomatoes in this section. Peppers share a lot of similarities to tomatoes in their growing preferences. Peppers like a pH level between 5.5 and 6.0 and a temperature in the range of warm to hot.

You can start peppers from seed or seedling. It takes about two to three months for your peppers to mature. When considering what kind of peppers to grow, know that jalapeno, habanero, mazurka, fellini, nairobi and cubico peppers all do fantastic in hydroponic growing.

Radishes

Like lettuce, radishes are one of the easiest plants to grow, whether it be in a traditional soil garden or in a hydroponic setup. As suggested in the last chapter, radishes are best grown from a seed rather than seedling and it only takes between three to seven days to begin seeing seedlings from them. Radishes grow well in a setup with lettuce because both plants like cool temperatures and a pH level between 6.0 and 7.0.

What's really good about radishes is that they don't need any lights, unlike most plants. This means that if the cost of getting a light is too much for you right out the gate, radishes offer a way of trying out hydroponic gardening before dropping that cash. What's craziest of all is that radishes can grow superfast, sometimes being ready to harvest within a month!

Spinach

Another plant that grows well in combination with lettuce and radishes is spinach. Spinach enjoys cool temperatures and a pH level between 6.0 and 7.0, so it fits in perfectly. It needs a little lighter than radishes do but it doesn't require very much at all.

It'll take about seven to ten days to go from seed to seedling with spinach and can be ready to harvest within six weeks. Harvesting can last up to twelve weeks depending on how you do. You can either harvest the spinach in full or you can pull off some leaves at a time. This makes spinach another great option for those first getting into hydroponic gardening.

Tomatoes

Okay, okay, we all know that tomatoes are technically a fruit. But we're looking at it here because together with the rest of the vegetables in this section, add tomatoes and you have one great salad! Tomatoes will grow best in a hot environment and you will want to set up a trellis in your grow tray. They also like a pH level between 5.5 and 6.5.

Tomatoes come in a variety; from the traditional ones we're looking at here through to those small cherry tomatoes that make delicious snacks. Germination can be expected between five to ten days and it will take a month or two before you begin to see fruit. You can expect it to take between fifty and a hundred days to be ready for harvesting and you will be able to tell by the size and color of the tomatoes.

Fruits

Nothing tastes sweeter than fruit that you have grown yourself. Hydroponic gardening offers a great way to grow some fruit inside the comfort of your own house. Like vegetables, there are many options available to us but we'll be focusing on those that grow the best.

Blueberries

Great for snacks, baking and even adding vitamins to your morning meal, blueberries are a fantastic crop to grow. However, blueberries can be quite difficult to germinate from seeds so it is recommended that you transplant blueberry plants instead. Blueberries are one of the slower plants to begin bearing fruit and can even take over a year to get to the point of producing. They like themselves a pH level between 4.5 and 6.0 in a warm climate.

Strawberries

The most popular of all the fruits that we can grow hydroponically, you can find strawberries being grown in smaller personal hydroponic setups and in the larger commercial growing operations. Preferring a warm temperature and a pH level of 6.0, strawberries grow best in a nutrient film technique system.

Strawberries that are grown from seeds can take up to three years to mature to harvesting levels, meaning that, like blueberries, they are a long-term crop. Together, blueberries and strawberries make for great fruit crops which can produce for several years if you are able to give them the growing time they need.

Herbs

Herbs make a great addition to any hydroponic setup. This is because it has been shown that herbs grown hydroponically have twenty to forty percent more aromatic oils than herbs that have been grown in a traditional soil garden. This means that you get more out of your hydroponic herbs with less used. This allows you to use less for the same end goal in your cooking, which means that your herbs will last you longer.

The best system for growing herbs is the ebb and flow system. Hydroponic herb gardens have been becoming a norm across the world because of their effectiveness. There are now even restaurants that grow their own hydroponic herb gardens on site because it is the most effective way to get fresh herbs of amazing quality.

Basil is the most popular of the herbs, with basil making up about 50% of the herb market in Europe. Both basil and mint like a warm environment and a pH level between 5.5 and 6.5. Similarly, chives prefer a warm to hot temperature and a pH sitting squarely around 6.0. This means that if you are careful with the temperature and pH level you can grow all three of these wonderful herbs in the same hydroponic setup.

An herb garden is a great way to get started with hydroponics. They can stay harvestable for incredibly long periods of time; they taste better than herbs grown in soil and make great additions to just about any meal. Not only that but herb gardens tend to be smaller than vegetable or fruit gardens and so a hydroponic herb garden will take up less space and can save some money in setup costs.

Hydroponic Nutrition

In this section, we'll turn our attention towards the nutrient solution which we use to fill up our reservoirs and provide our plants with what they need to continue to grow and stay strong. In order to get an understanding of this important component of our hydroponic systems, we will explore macro and micronutrients, the importance of researching the needs of our plants and how we go about mixing our own solution so that pH levels and electrical conductivity are in proper ratios.

What is a Nutrient Solution?

When we talk about the nutrient solution we use in our reservoirs, we are speaking about a properly proportioned liquid fertilizer. While there are a ton of commercial options available on the market today, we will be exploring how we go about mixing our own. This way, even if we decide to go with a store-bought option, we know how we can get the most control over our hydroponic garden's nutrition.

When it comes to growing plants, there are sixteen elements that combine together from the nutrients we use, our water and the oxygen in the air. A nutrient solution replaces those nutrients that would be found in the soil by combining them together into our water.

It is important to know what nutrients each of our plants want, as they are different from each other. There are more plants in this world than we can cover in one book, so it is important that you learn how to find this information for yourself. The best way to do this is to open up Google and search "name of plant + nutrient requirements hydroponic". If you were growing tomatoes then this would look like "tomato nutrient requirements hydroponic". Looking at the search results you will find that almost all of them are titled something like "Tomato fertilizer requirements" or "Tomato crop nutrition" and "What nutrients do tomato plants need?" Each of these sites will offer you the information you need. I recommend that you look at several sites rather than just one, to see if the needs change or if a particular site offers more specific information.

Primary Macronutrients

When we speak about primary macronutrients, we are referring to those nutrients that our plants require in large quantities. For humans, macronutrients are fat, protein and carbohydrates. While plants do care about these components, it is more for how they produce and handle them inside of themselves. When it comes to the nutrients they are after, our plants love nitrogen, phosphorus and potassium. We want to make sure that we have proper ratios of these big three so that our plants can stay at their healthiest, produce bigger yields and continue to grow.

Nitrogen

Found in amino acids, chlorophyll and nucleic acids, nitrogen is an element made up of enzymes and proteins. While humans like protein in its pure form, plants like it when they get it through nitrogen. If your plants aren't getting enough nitrogen then they will have a lower protein content. Too much nitrogen, on the other hand, leads to darker leaves and it adds to vegetative plant augmentation.

We want to make sure that our plants have a proper nitrogen balance because this will make sure that our plants are stronger, make better use of their own carbohydrates, stay healthier and manufacture more protein.

Phosphorus

Phosphorus is actually a major element in the RNA, DNA and ATP system of our plants. This is a lot of scientific jargon to say that phosphorus is super important to our plants. A deficiency of phosphorus can cause our plants to take longer to mature. Not only that but the poor plant growth and root growth can also lead to a reduced yield and see the plant's fruits drop off before they are mature. Likewise, too much phosphorus can lead to a lack of zinc (a micronutrient) in our plants.

Our plants want to be getting enough phosphorus so that they can better make use of photosynthesis. It also helps our plants in controlling cell division and in regulating how they make use of starches and sugars.

Potassium

The last of our three big macronutrients, potassium is slightly less important than nitrogen and phosphorus. This should not be taken as an excuse to ignore the potassium levels in our nutrient solutions. When our plants don't get enough potassium, they are at risk of having weaker stems and a reduced yield. Likewise, when we have too much potassium, we mess with the magnesium uptake of our plants.

When our plants are getting the right amount of potassium, we are making sure that they are using the water from our reservoirs to the best of their ability. Potassium also helps with our plants' resistance to disease, how they metabolize their nutrients and even how they regulate excess water.

Micronutrients

When we speak about micronutrients, we are referring primarily to seven different nutrients that our plants like to have. These are boron, chlorine, copper, iron, manganese, molybdenum and zinc. Together these micronutrients aren't nearly as important as our macronutrients but are still very important.

Typically, horticulturalists only add micronutrients when their plants show signs of some sort of deficiency. However, before you start adding micronutrients into your mixture, you want to make sure that the issue is actually with the nutrients themselves. For example, a deficiency can be caused by pests or poor pH levels. If we go adding micronutrients into our mixtures when the problem had nothing to do with the micronutrients, then we are risking damaging our plants. For this reason, you should first consider all the possible causes and rule out as many as you can before you start reaching for micronutrients.

Mixing Your Own Solution

The first thing we need to do when mixing our own solution is to figure out exactly what our plants need. We saw how we did this above in the section titled "What is a Nutrient Solution?" The information that you found in this section will let you know exactly what your plants want. We will take that information and use it here to fill out the specifics of this approach.

Before we get to mixing up our solution, we need to first go out and purchase some materials. We need to pick up some buckets. We need one bucket for each part of the solution. Three buckets tend to be a good number, as it allows us to tackle what they call an A, B, Bloom system. Some systems only require two buckets as there are only two steps to the mixture. You also want to buy a digital scale that can get down to hundredths of a gram. And of course, we need to purchase the nutrient salts that will be making up our solutions. These are salts which break down in water to give us the macronutrients we need. They can be bought at any hydroponic gardening store. Amazon.com also offers both premixed nutrient solutions and the raw nutrients you need to mix your own.

You will also want to make sure that you have some clean measuring cups and some rubber gloves to keep yourself safe. You want to fill the buckets up with the proper amount of water needed for each part of the solution. This will depend on what kind of mix your particular plants need and so will be a personalized amount. When it comes to our water, we need to make sure that it is clean. It is always better to use a filtration system to get rid of contaminants that may be present in the water.

You weigh out the proper amount of nutrient salt using the scale. Once you have this amount you pour the salt slowly into the first bucket of water. Do it slowly to stop it from splashing and losing some of the solution in the process. You should see the salts begin to dissolve almost as soon as they touch the water. After you finish the first one, measure out the salts for your second part of the solution. Repeat until all parts of the solution have been mixed in their own buckets. You may want to put lids on them and give them a shake to make sure that there are no clumps of nutrients left undissolved.

After we have our mixture (or mixtures) ready, we need to check the pH level. We know that most plants prefer something between 5.5 and 6.5. Water is a neutral medium which means that it has a pH level of 7. Get yourself some pH level testers and be prepared to get to work. We need to bring the level down a little bit. This means we have to adjust the pH level by mixing in a solution that is designed to lower the pH. These solutions are highly acidic, so you should only use a little bit at a time. You want to dilute the pH lower solution, so mix a couple of drops of it into a gallon of water. This should give you a solution closer to 2.0 or so. The nutrients you use raise the pH level of the water so you need to start from 2.0 and increase as you add the mixture. You then slowly add this diluted mixture into your nutrient solution. Make sure that you add this slowly and stop to check the pH level often.

After your pH level is in line, you will need to check the electrical conductivity of the mixture. To do this you need to get yourself an electronic EC meter. Electrical conductivity lets us get an accurate reading of the balance of nutrients and pH level. Since we have mixed our own nutrient solution, we have had to use mineral salts to get the nutrients we desire. We can figure out the number of nutrients in the solution through electrical conductivity. Most plants want an EC of somewhere between 1.5 and 2.5 so this can be a great way to check and make sure we've got a proper mixture before we feed it off to our plants.

If we come in lower than 1.5, this means we don't have enough nutrients in our solution and so we will need to add more in order to bring it up. Likewise, if it is too high then we risk subjecting our plants to nutrient burn. Nutrient burn refers to the physical signs that our plants are getting too many nutrients. Leaf scorch is an obvious sign of nutrient burn. Root burn is also another common symptom of nutrient burn. We want to raise healthy plants, so this means we shouldn't be overfeeding them too many nutrients.

Once you've checked to see that the EC level is where you want it, you have successfully mixed your own nutrient solution. While the specifics depend on the plants you choose to grow, this outline should show you that it really isn't that hard to prepare our own solutions and keep close control over our hydroponic systems and the health of our plants.

Chapter Summary

- We have a ton of options available to us when it comes to growing vegetables including beans, cucumbers, kale, lettuce, peppers, radishes, spinach and tomatoes.

- When it comes to fruits, blueberries and strawberries make great additions to a hydroponic garden.

- Herbs grow amazingly in hydroponic gardens, having up to forty percent more aromatic oils than soil-grown herbs. The most popular of these is basil but many herbs grow especially well in an ebb and flow system.

- A nutrient solution is a properly proportioned liquid fertilizer that we can either buy from the store or we can mix ourselves.

- When it comes to our plants, they want a lot of macronutrients. This macronutrient food group is made up of nitrogen, phosphorus and potassium.

- Micronutrients for plants are boron, chlorine, copper, iron, manganese, molybdenum and zinc. Before we start introducing micronutrients into our nutrient solutions, we should first take steps to make sure that the problem is actually related to a lack of micronutrients.

- We want to make sure of this because we want to avoid subjecting our plants to nutrient burn, which is what happens when they have too many nutrients and it can really hurt their overall health.

- Always use filtered water and wear rubber gloves when you are mixing your own solution. For each step in your solution, use a separate bucket that you have sterilized.

- After you mix in your nutrient salts, check the pH level of the water. Most plants prefer a pH level between 5.5 and 6.5.

- The last step is to check the EC level of our solution. We want an EC level somewhere between 1.5 and 2.5.

In the next chapter, you will learn all about how to keep your hydroponic garden in great working order through regular check-ups and maintenance. This includes sanitizing and sterilizing your equipment and trays. You'll see how we keep our reservoirs clean and clear of any problems. We'll look at root disease and how to handle salt build-up before it kills off your plants. You'll learn how to tell when algae becoming a problem and when to clean it out and you'll learn all about problems with fruiting and flowering.

CHAPTER FIVE

MAINTENANCE OF YOUR HYDROPONIC GARDEN

By this point, we have made our hydroponic systems, picked out the plants we want to grow and mixed together a batch of nutrient solution to give them all the macronutrients they could ever desire. By now, it is safe to call yourself a hydroponic gardener! But the work hasn't finished yet. Now that you have your setup and you are growing your plants; you have to remain vigilant in maintaining your hydroponic garden.

This chapter is packed full of tools to help make sure that your garden continues to run smoothly. To this end, we'll look at how we sanitize our growing space, as well as how we go about sterilizing it. These two words are often used interchangeably but are actually two different steps. From there will explore the ways we can keep our reservoirs in good condition, look at some general troubleshooting advice and speak on how our plants tell us that they need help. Because of how super important the information in this section is, we will close out the sections with a quick recap on the actions you should be taking for your garden.

Sanitizing

When it comes to sanitizing our hydroponic gardens, what we mean is that we are giving our garden a deep clean. It is as important to keep our gardens clean as changing a burnt-out lightbulb is or making sure that our nutrient solution is properly balanced. A proper sanitization will kill off and get rid of most microorganisms that can cause damage. Sanitizing doesn't mean that you are using a cleaning product or a chemical solution. While this can be a part of sanitizing, sanitizing can be as simple as a wipe down and the removal of any filth and dead plant matter.

The first step in sanitizing which you will want to take is to make sure that any spills, excess water or plant runoff is immediately cleaned up. You can purchase a wet/dry vacuum which can help in cleaning up spills but, while this is a useful tool, you can do this cleaning by hand as well. You want to make sure that you are getting these spills quickly and cleaning them up fully because the extra moisture on the floor can raise the room's humidity. A rise in humidity increases the risk that mold will take up residence in our systems. It also risks exposing our plants to rot, which is a plant's worst nightmare. Not only that, but spills can actually damage your floors which can lead to having to pay for repairs.

Any time you enter into the room in which you keep your hydroponic garden, you want to keep an eye out for any dead plant matter that you can find. You should take the time every day to check for fallen leaves and other dead plant matter. While it is easy to just check your grow tray and call it a day, make sure you check the floor around your garden as plant matter can easily escape and out of sight doesn't mean it isn't hurting your plants. These will fall into your grow tray or onto the floor around your garden. We want to clean up this dead plant matter because it is extremely enticing to mold and fungi. It is also extremely enticing to a variety of pests (we'll see how to deal with those in the next chapter). Make sure when you harvest your crops that you always get rid of old root and plant matter rather than leave it for later.

When it comes to facing problems with plant rot, a lot of gardeners never realize that the problem stems from the cleanliness of the grow room. In the last chapter, we saw that we want to make sure that the problem with our plants is not something else before we start adding micronutrients into our solutions. This is one of those situations where people jump to conclusions. However, one of the first things we should be checking is that we have kept a clean garden space.

If your hydroponic setup uses an intake filter, then you are going to want to inspect and clean that filter at least once a week or so. These filters help to keep dust, bugs and molds from getting into our growing trays. Routine cleaning of the intake filter will make sure that your system keeps maximum airflow. It will also be a way to get an early warning of any pests that are trying to get into your garden. Finding a pest on the intake filter gives you a head start on preventing them from messing up and damaging your garden.

Once every few months or so you should also take out the bulbs from your lights and give them a wipe. You should also do this with any glass you have such as when you use a reflector with your lights. Setting a schedule to do this, say, every three months, will allow you to plan it out ahead of time and to make sure that you don't neglect this cleaning. Harvesting can also be a great time to get at this cleaning, as when we harvest our plants, we tend to open up more space and make it easier to get at our equipment. Glass cleaners or isopropyl alcohol can be used to clean this glass. We want to keep up with this cleaning as grime can build up on our glass and lights and this can reduce the light output that we are able to give our plants.

You will also want to sanitize the hardware in your grow room about as often as you clean the glass. This means wiping down our pumps, hoses, all the stuff like that. You'll even want to wipe down the outside of your grow tray and your reservoir. If you have equipment that has exposed circuitry then you will want to get a couple of cans of compressed air so that you can clean these without damaging any of the electronics.

To recap: Clean up any spills as soon as they happen. Check for dead plant material once a day. Check your intake filters on a weekly basis. Every couple of months you should get in and clean the glass and bulbs used in your lighting setup. Around the time you clean your glass, you should also give any hardware you are using a quick clean, using compressed air on anything with exposed circuitry.

Sterilization

When it comes to cleaning, sterilization is a more involved process than sanitization is. We sterilize our equipment in order to kill off microorganisms like bacteria, spores and fungi. Because we are speaking on hydroponic systems with the assumption that they will be kept indoors, we will look at how we use chemical cleaners to sterilize our equipment. We can also use heat and filtration but these are more involved and complicated and are more useful for large-scale growing operations.

Unlike sanitization, we don't want to sterilize nearly as often. With sanitization, some of the practices are best used on a daily or a weekly basis. Sterilization should be used far less often because not only is it unnecessary but it can also hurt our system and our plants. For one, it takes more time and thought to sterilize and it can leave nasty by-products if we aren't careful to rinse properly afterward. When it comes to sterilization, we will be primarily looking at sterilizing our trays and reservoir, as well as the inside of any tubes we must clean.

The two most common chemical cleaners for sterilization are bleach and hydrogen peroxide. Bleach typically contains sodium hypochlorite as its active ingredient. This is the same chemical which is used to disinfect wastewater. While bleach makes for a great sterilizer, it can leave residual traces on our equipment and so if you choose to use bleach you should be prepared to double and triple rinse anything you cleaned using it. After you harvest your plants but before you set up the next batch to grow is a great time for a bleach bath. Using a mixture of one-part bleach to one part water, you should soak any air stones or other submersibles as well as your tray and reservoir. Make sure that you rinse these off two or three times, just to be extra sure that no harmful residue is left.

Hydrogen peroxide is actually just water that has an unstable oxygen molecule. This makes it a great chemical cleaner as instead of leaving behind a harmful residue it actually breaks down into water. Since water doesn't hurt our plants, using hydrogen peroxide means you don't have to worry as much about the double or triple rinsing that bleach requires. You can use a rag that has been soaked in 3% hydrogen peroxide to wipe down and clean your components. If you have a larger setup, you may consider creating a hydrogen peroxide solution that you can have run through the system. For this, you would want to keep it at about 35% hydrogen peroxide. If you run a hydrogen peroxide mix through your system, make sure that you send some water through to rinse afterward before you return your plants to the system.

To recap: You shouldn't sterilize too often as this can hurt your plants. A good time to sterilize is between harvesting and setting up the new crop. If you use bleach to sterilize, make sure you double or triple rinse afterward to prevent residue from hurting your plants.

Maintaining Your Reservoir

When it comes to our gardens, it is clear that we have a favorite section. All the greenery at the top is just so pretty and exciting to watch grow. It can be easy to maintain a habit of removing the dead leaves that have fallen because it is fun to poke around our plants and see how they are doing. But while it is easy to focus up top, we can't let ourselves forget about how important the bottom of our system is too. Without the reservoir of nutrient solution, our plants wouldn't get what they need to grow and we would just have one dead garden.

Our reservoirs are such an important part of our hydroponic systems that we should make it our mission to see that they are kept in the best possible shape. To do that, there are several steps and behaviors that we should adapt to make sure we stay on top of reservoir maintenance.

The first step we should take is making sure that our reservoirs are kept at a proper temperature. If we let our reservoirs get too hot then the levels of oxygen go down and create conditions for root rot to flourish. We want to keep our nutrient solution around 65-75 degrees. If our reservoirs are too cold, we can always get an aquarium heater or a heating pad to raise the temperature up. If our reservoirs are too hot then there are several options available to us. We can get a reservoir chiller, move our setups into the shade, or add some ice cubes to our solution. We also want to make sure that after we paint our reservoir black, we then add a coat of white paint to help reflect rather than absorb heat.

If your hydroponic garden is using a circulating system, then you are going to need to make sure that you check on your water levels and top up the reservoir. We lose water to evaporation and to processes that our plants undergo. This means that water loss is a part of the gardening experience and so we should be prepared to top up what is lost. This is especially important with smaller systems, as the loss of a little bit of water in a smaller system is a bigger deal.

Once every week or every other week you should consider changing out the water in your reservoir. This is a process that can get very specific for each garden. Knowing when it is time to change is something that you will grow into. But to start, assume every two weeks. Using your EC meter can help you to know when the time is right. While the EC reader will let us know how much fertilizer is in our solutions, it doesn't give us a breakdown of how much of each nutrient is left. Our plants don't use every nutrient the same way, some are absorbed and processed quicker than others. This means that even when we are checking levels with our EC meter and seeing that there are enough nutrients, we can actually have too much of one kind and not enough of another. When we change out our water, we are able to make sure that we provide our plants with a freshly balanced nutrient solution. It also gives us a chance to sanitize our reservoirs.

Speaking of our EC meters, we want to make sure we are doing regular EC checks. Of course, the numbers we are aiming for here depend on what plants we are growing. By this point, you should already have researched proper EC levels for your plant of choice. You also want to make sure to do regular pH level checks. We know that we want to keep our pH around roughly 5.5 to 6.5.

Finally, the most important step of all is to make sure you are checking your pumps regularly. You want to get on top of any build-ups that may be growing in your pumps. We want to do this because nothing kills off a garden faster than a broken pump. Making sure to clean out your pumps and clear away any nutrient build-ups will go a long way to keeping your garden healthy and keeping your reservoir working as intended.

To recap: Keep your reservoir between 65-75 degrees. Check the water levels and top them up often. Change the water out of your reservoir every other week. Use an EC meter and pH tests to keep your levels in check. Check your pumps regularly to prevent blockages.

Salt Build-up and Salt Burn

Have you ever seen a garden that has a white (or off-white) build-up of crystalline crust on the stems of the plants or the top of the growing medium? This is what is called a salt build-up and it is very bad for your plants. A salt build-up can lead to salt burn. Salt burn around the roots will lead to the stem at the base of the plant dying. This leads to wilting during the hotter moments of the day and it can even open this area of your plant up as the perfect feasting ground for disease.

Salt build-up happens when your growing medium loses moisture to evaporation at a faster rate than the plants are able to use up the nutrients. The moisture evaporates but the nutrients stay behind and jack up the EC levels in the medium. The good news is that salt build-up is easy to handle as long as you know that's what you're dealing with.

That white crust on the stems and top of your growing medium is a dead giveaway. If you are seeing that white crust and you notice that your plants have become stunted in their growth, have taken on a darker color or are growing uncharacteristically slow, then you should have all the signs you need to diagnose a salt build-up. One way you can confirm your suspicions is to take an EC reading of the solution that drains from your growing tray. If the EC reading increases on draining, you almost certainly have a salt build-up problem.

If you have identified a salt build-up as a problem in your garden, then you are going to want to flush your growing media. While some gardeners will flush their system with plain water, this can actually have a negative effect. If there is a crop already growing, the drop in osmotic pressure can cause the plants to take in a ton of moisture around the roots. This can lead to fruit splitting or the vegetative growth coming in soft and weak.

A healthier approach to flushing the growing medium is to use a flushing solution that has been premixed, such as you can find at any hydroponic store. You can also flush with a nutrient solution that is at one third the regular strength. Depending on your setup, you may find yourself needing to do this flush every few weeks such as if you have an ebb and flow system in a warm climate where evaporation happens easily.

To recap: You can identify salt build-up by a white crust on the top of your grow medium and on the bottom of your plant stems. This happens because of evaporation that leaves the nutrients stuck there. Use a nutrient solution flush at one-third of regular strength in order to clear away the build-up.

Algae

If you are running a hydroponic garden, you will have to deal with algae at some point, I promise. Therefore, it is important that you know what to keep a lookout for. Algae will look like a slimy growth that clings onto the different parts of your setup. It can be brown, green, reddish or black. You shouldn't be surprised if you find long strings of algae in your system and you shouldn't be surprised if it seems like it just showed up out of nowhere. Algae can grow super-fast.

Algae also smells horrible. It has a moldy, earthy scent to it. When you get a ton of algae decomposing in your system, it will give off an unpleasant odor that can be a sign that you have a serious algae build-up on your hands.

Algae can be a real pain. First off, it is really quite disgusting looking. But far worse than its esthetical value and its smell is the fact that algae can easily block up your drippers, pumps and any other component of your hydroponic system that is prone to blockages. Like we saw, this can easily kill off your garden. Not only that but if you have a serious algae problem it can even block off your growing substrates and steal oxygen away from your plants. When this starts to happen, it can lead to an increase in the biological oxygen demand of your system. This means that your plants won't be getting enough oxygen and this can lead to their roots suffocating. If algae attach directly to your plants' roots, then it can leave your plants at risk for pathogens like Pythium.

Algae itself can really suck but it gets even worse when it begins to break down and decompose. When this happens, it can actually release toxins into your system. These toxins then act as a food source for pathogenic fungi. When this begins to happen fungi can seem to just suddenly pop up and get a strong foothold in your system.

Most hydroponic growers tolerate a small number of algae in their systems because it can be difficult to get rid of. If you are taking care of your reservoir and making sure to clean it, then you can also take care of algae at this point. Make sure that you scrub down your systems between grows so that any algae that has gotten a foothold is removed. Some growers will use algaecide products in their nutrient solution to kill off algae but this can also cause our plants to be damaged. Not only that but algae regrow quite quickly after the use of algaecide products. This means that you will have to add in more algaecide soon afterward, thus risking your plants' health yet again.

To recap: A little bit of algae is fine but a major problem needs to be handled before it decomposes or it blocks up pumps and working components of your system. Clean by hand rather than using algaecides.

Maintaining Root Health

When it comes to the health of our roots, the most common killers are starvation, suffocation, damage from chemicals, pathogens, temperature or the EC/pH levels. The leading cause of root death and poor growing rates is suffocation. Many pathogens won't attack a healthy root system until they have been damaged due to poor conditions. Suffocation happens when there is a lack of oxygen getting to the plants such as when there is too much decomposing organic matter in our reservoirs, slow flow rates or too many plants all fighting to get enough oxygen.

As the roots begin to suffocate due to lack of oxygen, toxins will start to proliferate. Some plants will try to grow new roots to find alternative sources of oxygen but many will just up and die. If your plants aren't getting enough oxygen, consider adding an oxygen stone to your reservoir.

If there aren't enough nutrients moving through your system, this will have an effect on the root system the same way that it affects the top part of the plant. However, it can be harder to tell that there is an issue with the roots. A lack of phosphate will cause the roots to turn brown and you will see a reduction in the number of lateral branches. A calcium deficiency causes the root system to thin out and develop a sickly brown color. Lack of manganese will lead to a root system that is shorter and finer than normal and you'll notice the tips of the roots browning. These each are clues that you want to take care of your nutrient solution and reservoir.

Another thing can lead to damaging our plants' roots are improperly balanced EC and pH levels. An unbalanced system will lead to severe stunting of the roots. At higher EC levels water will be lost from the roots and lead to root death. This is a common response from plants that enjoy a lower EC level. When pH levels get to be too high or too low then we can see root damage and problems with nutrient uptake. However, plants will take much kindlier to fluctuations in pH levels than they will in EC levels.

When it comes to root diseases, setups that use a recirculating system for the nutrient solution present the most risk. This is because the circulating of the solution can easily carry pathogens through to all of our plants. Some pathogens will attack the roots in a hydroponic system in a way that makes them easy to identify while others will seem almost invisible. Regardless if they show or not, all pathogens will lead to a reduction in the growth of your plants and the amount they yield. The most common pathogens that mess with our roots are didymella, verticillium, olpidium, plasmopara, pythium, fusarium and phytophthora.

Pathogens that affect your roots can come from a variety of sources. They can be airborne, waterborne, found in your growing medium, arrive from insects and pests, infected plant matter or even from seeds and dust. While airborne pathogens that damage your roots are rare, they can still happen. One of the most common sources for infection comes from soil. Soil can get into a hydroponic system from your hands, shoes, dust in the air, from our equipment or even from the water we use in our reservoir.

Root diseases and the pathogens that cause them like to attack plants that are already undergoing a lot of stress. Because stressed plants leave your system open to attack, the best way to defend against these pathogens is to make sure that your crop is healthy and not undergoing undue stress such as when we trim stems too often. Another cause of stress is our roots not getting enough oxygen, such as when algae has grown into a major problem.

One of the best behaviors we can get into is making sure that we take the time to check on the root system of our plants. Most of us want to poke around on the top part where it's all green and pretty. While it is important that we take care of our tops, we must not forget the bottom. Checking the roots on a regular basis will be a great tool for catching a problem before it becomes a crisis. If your plant is wilting or looks discolored then you should make sure to check the root system.

If you identify that a plant has or potentially has root disease, then your first step should be to remove it from the garden and destroy it. If a plant is diseased and you leave it in the system, you risk that disease being carried to the other healthy plants. These pathogens can survive and go from one crop to the next, so it is important that you sanitize and sterilize your hydroponic system between crops.

To recap: Root health is just as important as the health of our tops. A lack of oxygen is the most common problem for our roots. Avoid stressing the plants by doing regular checks of the EC and pH levels. Identify issues with roots so that you can remove diseased plants before they spread to healthy plants.

Fruiting and Flowering

When it comes to problems with our crops fruiting and flowering there can be a lot of different causes. These range from a lack of fruit development through to physiological disorders such as blossom end rot. You may find your fruits have skin disorders like blotches, streaks, silvering or uneven color. Another issue is fruit splitting which leads to ugly looking plants that are horribly misshapen.

Many hydroponic crops will begin to flower and fruit when they reach a proper age. If there is a problem with the fruiting, you may run into a problem with flower dropping. This is when the flowers and fruits drop off the plant before they are ready. This can be caused by external problems but it can also be internal such as when our plants are undergoing an undue amount of stress. A lot of crops will run into flower drop if the air temperatures are too high. The point at which heat affects plants is different for each kind. If your plants aren't getting enough light, this can also lead to flower drop. A lack of light also can stunt the growth of the whole plant.

Flower drop can also be caused by nutrient deficiencies. Common causes of flower drop due to deficiency are when our plants aren't getting enough nitrogen or phosphorus from the nutrient solution we have made. Stress caused by water can also lead to flower drop. This is stress caused by a poor irrigation system or from having an EC level that is too high. For this reason, we want to make sure that we are checking the EC levels of our nutrient solutions on a regular basis.

Another cause of fruit drop is when the weight of the fruit is too heavy for the plant to hold onto. This can be due to the weight of the fruit or the weight of the vegetative growth itself. For this reason, we want to make sure that we are trimming our plants in a healthy manner that promotes a manageable growth such as when we top our plants. When there are larger fruits growing on our plants, this can lead to the dropping of smaller fruits. This can actually serve to help the healthier, larger fruits to continue growing. Likewise, we may consider removing smaller fruits so that the energy spent growing them is redirected.

To recap: Issues with flowering and fruiting tend to be related to stress. Make sure to take good care of your plants, remove unhealthy fruits and give heavy plants support to prevent dropping.

Chapter Summary

- Sanitizing refers to giving our systems a deep clean.

- Clean any spills as soon as they happen to prevent the moisture from messing with the room's humidity.

- Check for dead plant matter daily. This matter becomes a breeding ground for molds, fungi and bacteria.

- Clean your intake filter once a week or so to keep them in working order and get early warnings about possible pests.

- Every few months clean the bulbs and glass used in your lighting setup.

- Clean down your pumps, hoses and other hardware when you clean your bulbs.

- Sterilization is a more involved process but shouldn't be overused as it can damage your plants.

- Bleach and hydrogen peroxide can both be used to sterilize. If you use bleach make sure you double and triple rinse to remove all harmful residue.

- Make sure that you keep your reservoir at a temperature of between 65-75 degrees.

- Top off the water levels in your reservoir as they get lower.

- Change the water in your reservoir every other week to keep tight control over the amount of nutrients in your solutions.

- Do regular EC and pH level checks.

- Check your pumps often to avoid blockages and breakdowns.

- Salt build-up can be identified by a layer of white crust on the top of your growing medium and the stems of your plants.

- Salt build-up happens when water evaporates from our solution and leaves its nutrients to build up.

- Salt build-up can lead to salt burn which can kill off parts of our plants and leave them at risk of pathogens.

- To deal with a salt build-up, flush your system with a nutrient solution at one-third of its regular strength.

- Algae is a disgusting smelling, slimy growth (that can be green, red, black or brown) that grows in your reservoir.

- A serious algae problem can block up pumps and drippers and rotting algae can release toxins into your system.

- A small number of algae is typical in a hydroponic system, just make sure you scrub down and remove any algae every so often.

- You can use algaecide products to kill off the algae but this can also hurt your plants so if it isn't a huge build-up it can be best to wait until the next time you clean your reservoir.

- The most common cause of root damage is suffocation from a lack of oxygen.

- A lack of properly balanced nutrients will hurt your plants' roots just as much as it will hurt the tops.

- Improper EC and pH levels can also lead to root death, so make sure to keep an eye on your levels.

- Recirculating systems are at a bigger risk of spreading root-based diseases among your plants.

- Be careful about how much dirt is in your hands and clothing when you look after your garden as this is the key way for pathogens to get into your system.

- Root disease prefers to attack plants already under a lot of stress, so the best way to prevent root disease is to take proper care of your plants.

- Make sure you check your roots often and remove and destroy any plant showing signs of root disease.

- Pathogens can survive from one crop to the next, so always sterilize between crops.

- If there is a problem with fruiting, you may see flower dropping or fruit splitting.

- The most common cause of these fruiting problems is stressed out plants.

- Nutrient deficiencies can also be responsible for flower drop.

- Flower and fruit drop can also be caused by the weight of the fruit, so a trellis can help prevent this.

In the next chapter, you will learn all about the different kinds of pests that can try to take up a foothold in your garden. Along with a look at the pests themselves, you will learn how we take care of them so that we can keep our hydroponic gardens in the best shape possible.

CHAPTER SIX

PEST CONTROL

We've made it through setting up our own hydroponic garden, picking plants, learning about nutrients and figuring out how we can maintain it. But now we've come across a whole new issue: Pests. Our setup provided a great environment for our plants to grow. But it also created an environment which pests love and we even filled it with tons of healthy plants for them to eat. This would be fine if they provided some kind of service to our plants but all they want to do is snack on them and leave them wilted and yellowed.

In this chapter, we'll take a look at the most common pests that hydroponic growers encounter and we'll see how you can spot them in your own garden. Our number one defense against pests is to prevent them from making our gardens their home in the first place, so we will learn some of the techniques used to detect them early and prevent an infestation.

113

Pests aren't the only problem we face as hydroponic growers. Disease is also something we must be vigilant in spotting, identifying and handling. To this end, we'll look at some of the more common diseases and how we can prevent them. A lot of this information was covered in chapter five, so we will be referring to it often here.

Common Hydroponic Pests

While there are many pests that can try to make our gardens their home, there are certain pests that show up with more regularity than others. These pests fall into five key categories: spider mites, thrips, fungus gnats, whiteflies and aphids. If you find yourself with an infestation of pests, it is a safe bet that they'll fall into one of these five categories.

Spider Mites

Out of all five types of pest, spider mites are a particularly annoying one. While they are less than a millimeter long, these little guys are actually tiny spiders. Because they are so small, they have a tendency to start damaging your plants before you even notice that they have taken up in your garden.

Spider mite damage will look like tiny brown and yellow spots on the leaves of your plants. While they don't look like anything serious when there are only a couple of bites, this damage adds up quickly to really wreak havoc on your garden.

To spot a spider mite infestation, there are two key signs to look out for. While the damage on your plants can be a telltale sign, it doesn't specifically tell you that spider mites are the problem. To spot a spider mite infestation you should check your plants to see if you can spot any spider-like webbing. Another way to check for spider mites is to use a tissue or clean rag to gently wipe the bottoms of your leaves. If you come away with streaks of blood, this will tell you that you have a spider mite problem.

One way of handling spider mites is to wash your plants down with a hose or powerful spray bottle. The force of the water can often knock the mites off of your plant and drown them in the growing medium. Spider mites also have some natural enemies ranging from ladybugs to lacewings and you may consider adding these beneficial insects to your garden to feed on the spider mite population.

Aphids

These little guys are also known as plant lice. And just like head lice, they aren't all that much fun. These tiny, soft-bodied pests are pretty much able to set up in any environment. They multiply quicker than rabbits, so you want to make sure to tackle an aphid infestation as soon as possible. These pests are typically a quarter of an inch in size and can come in green, yellow, pink, black or gray varieties.

Aphids like to feed on the juices of the plant and you can find them chewing on stems, leaves, buds, fruits or roots. They are particularly drawn to the newest parts of the plant. If you find that your leaves are misshapen or yellowing, checking the bottom can reveal aphids. They also leave behind a sticky substance referred to as honeydew. This sweet substance can actually attract other kinds of pests so aphids are particularly annoying little critters. This substance can also lead to the growth of fungus, like sooty mold which can cause your branches or leaves to turn an unpleasant black color. Aphids are also able to carry viruses from one plant to another so they can help nasty pathogens to spread quicker.

Like spider mites, spraying water on the leaves can dislodge them and leave them with a hard time finding their way back to your plants. If the infestation is large, dusting your plants with flour can constipate them and help convince them it is time to move on. Wiping down your plants with a mixture of soapy water can also help to kill and drive them off.

Thrips

Like spider mites and aphids, these little guys are also tiny. Often, they are only around 5 millimeters long. It can be hard to spot these little guys but they leave damage that is clear as day. If you start to see little metallic black specks on your leaves, you probably have some thrips snacking off your garden. Leaves that thrips attack will often turn brown and become super dry because the thrips like to suck out their juices.

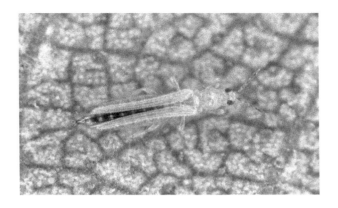

Thrips are small and are either black or the color of straw. They have slender bodies and two pairs of wings. Because they are so small, they look like dark threads to the naked eye. They like to feed in large groups and will fly away if you disturb them. They stick their eggs into flowers and leaves and they only take a couple of days to hatch so a thrip infestation can feel like it just happened out of the blue.

Because thrips like to lay their eggs in plants, it is super important that you remove any dead or fallen plant matter. If you paid attention in the last chapter, you'll know you should be doing this anyway as it helps to prevent many issues that can assail our hydroponic gardens. Make sure that you inspect your plants for thrip damage and remove any that are infested. Hosing off the plants will also help to reduce their population. Ladybugs, lacewings and minute pirate bugs all feed on thrips and can be beneficial to your garden.

Fungus Gnats

Fungus gnats are an odd one. Adult fungus gnats have no interest in harming your garden. But their larvae enjoy chewing on the roots of your plants which slows growth and opens the plant up for infection. In extreme cases, fungus gnat larvae can actually cause the death of plants. They really like areas with a lot of moisture and a high humidity. You'll likely notice adult fungus gnats before you have any issue. As adults, these gnats are about three millimeters in length and kind of look like mosquitos. They tend to be a grayish-black color with a pair of long legs and clear wings. Their larvae have shiny black heads with a whitish-transparent body.

Adults typically live for a week and in that time lay up to 300 eggs. It takes half a week for the larvae to emerge but when they do, they start a two-week diet where their main dish is the roots of your plants. When they feed on your plants, they cause them to wilt, stunt their growth and cause a yellowing of their leaves. These nasty little things can have many generations living off the same plant.

If you suspect a fungus gnat infestation than you should inspect your plants by carefully turning up the soil around their stems and look for larvae. If you check a plant and it suddenly let's loose a bunch of adult gnats then you should dispose of that plant. They really like damp soils so make sure you aren't overwatering your plants. If you have a fungus gnat problem then letting your potting medium drain longer will help to kill off the larvae and mess up the development of fungus gnat eggs. You can also spray your plants with a combination of peppermint, cinnamon and sesame oils. This mixture is called flying insect killer and will help to get rid of gnats.

Whiteflies

About the same size as spider mites, whiteflies look like small white moths that take up residence on your plants. They are easier to spot but because they fly away when you bother them they can be hard to kill. Like aphids, they enjoy sucking the juices out of your plant and you see their damage as white spots and yellowing of the leaves.

They tend to lay 200-400 eggs in clusters on the underside of the higher leaves. These eggs hatch in about a week and unattractive little nymphs come out that crawl around on your leaves before they grow wings. These crawlers will spread out from the egg and find a place to start chewing on your leaves. They'll stay in that spot for the next week or so before growing into young adults which will repeat the cycle of movement-feasting.

Ladybugs and lacewings enjoy eating whiteflies and so introducing them to your garden can help to kill off whitefly populations. Hosing off plants with a strong blast of water will help in reducing their numbers as well. There are a bunch of organic pesticides on the market which you can get to deal with whiteflies. These pesticides can also work for the other pests but pesticides should be a last resort option, one that you are careful with so as not to lead to undue stress on your plants.

Preventing Pests

Now that we have an idea of the pests that are most common to hydroponic gardens, let us turn our attention towards how we prevent these pests from getting into our gardens in the first place. Many of these techniques will help us to identify a possible infestation as it is trying to get started and so they offer us early warnings to prepare ourselves to battle pests. If we keep up our preventative measures and keep our eyes peeled for pests then we can save our plants a lot of damage and ourselves a lot of time by cutting off the problem at the head.

When it comes to pests it is also important to understand that not every pest is the same. This doesn't just mean that whiteflies are different from fungus gnats. What this means is that fungus gnats on the West coast are going to be different than fungus gnats on the East coast. Not every solution for prevention or extermination will work. A certain pesticide may be used to kill gnats on the East but the ones on the West might have grown an immunity to it. For this reason, it is important to check with your local hydroponics store to see if there is any region-specific information you need to tackle your pest problem.

One of the ways that we prevent pests is to make sure that we limit their ability to enter our garden in the first place. We can do this a few ways. Insect screens go a long way to keeping out pests. We also want to limit the amount of traffic in and around our setups. If at all possible, our setups will benefit greatly if they can be protected by airlock entrances as these offer the most secure protection against both pests and pathogens. Airlocks can be doubled up to create a space before the garden in which to wipe down dirt and any insects or eggs that are catching a free ride on your clothing.

In order to see if pests are starting to show up in your garden, use sticky traps around your plants. Yellow and blue sticky traps are both useful, as they attract different pests, so you want to make sure to use both kinds for the best results. Place traps near any entrances into your garden such as doors or ventilation systems. Also, make sure to place one or two near the stems of your plants to catch those pests that prefer snacking on the lower bits, such as aphids or fungus gnats. Get into the habit of checking these traps regularly as they can give you a great idea of what kind of life is calling your garden home.

While traps will help us to get a head start fighting any infections, they aren't a foolproof method when it comes to avoiding pests. Traps should be used together with personal spot checks.

This means that you should be checking your plants for pests a couple of times a week. Take a clean cloth and check the bottom of your leaves. Check around the roots for any fungus gnat larvae. You can check the tops of leaves visually. Look for any signs of yellowing or bite marks as described above.

Make sure to remove any weeds that take up root in your garden as these plants are only going to sap your garden's resources and offer a breeding ground for pests. Also remove dead or fallen plant matter, of course. This includes leaves but also any fruit, buds or petals that have been dropped.

Finally, before you introduce any new plants to your garden, make sure to quarantine them first so that you can check them for pests. You can use a magnifying glass to get a closer look if you need to. Give the new plants a thorough inspection, making sure to check all parts of the plant and the potting soil before you transfer it over.

By creating a system and a schedule for inspecting your plants, you can prevent an infestation of pests from ruining your garden or causing you a lot of headaches. A vigilant eye will give you the upper hand in both preventing and dealing with any kind of problem you have with pests. Remember, a strong defense is the best offense when it comes to keeping your plants healthy and free from harm.

Common Hydroponic Diseases

Disease is awful whether we're speaking about humans or about our plants. In the last chapter, we saw how we maintain a healthy garden so as to prevent pathogens from taking hold in our systems. Here we will look at the most common diseases that hydroponic growers find themselves facing.

Iron Deficiency

When your plants don't get enough iron they won't be able to produce enough chlorophyll. This means that their leaves will turn bright yellow with bold green veins. If left untreated, the leaves will start to turn white and then begin to die. This will result in a stunting of growth and a dying back of the plant as a whole. These signs of iron deficiency look a lot like some of the other diseases so it is important that you confirm it is an iron deficiency before you begin treatment.

To diagnose an iron deficiency, you are going to want to test your growing operation. Do a pH test and check the numbers. Higher than 7.0 can cause many plants to stop absorbing iron. Also, do an EC reading and check your levels; you may have an imbalance. Remember that an EC check doesn't confirm how many of each nutrient is in your solution so you may consider changing out the nutrient solution for a freshly balanced batch.

If you have identified an iron deficiency, the first thing you should do is fix the pH and EC levels and get that all within the proper range. You can also buy liquid iron which you use to spray down your plants. Spray the liquid iron directly on the leaves. Liquid iron is only a quick fix and not the solution, so if it shows results then consider tweaking your nutrient solution to include more iron.

Powdery Mildew

Powdery mildew is an easily recognizable fungal disease. Caused by fungal species, this disease thrives on plants in areas with less moisture in the growing medium and it especially loves it when the humidity levels are high on the surface of your plants. This mildew begins on the younger leaves of plants and it looks like little blisters all over them. These blisters are slightly raised and they lead to your leaves curling up. This curling exposes the lower parts of the leaf's structure for easier access. Leaves that have been infected look like they are coated in an unsightly white powder. Left untreated the leaves will turn brown and fall off. It primarily attacks new leaves and so the older, more mature leaves of your plant will tend to be free of infection.

To deal with powdery mildew, you want to prune away some of the plant to open it up to better airflow. This will help to reduce the humidity of the plant so as to make it less inviting to powdery mildew. Remove any foliage that is already infected and make sure to clean up any fallen plant matter. A spray made of 60% water and 40% milk can be used once every two weeks to help prevent powdery mildew from taking hold. Also wash your plants from time to time, as this will help prevent both powdery mildew and a variety of pests. A fungicide can be applied if the problem is extreme but this also risks hurting the plants.

Gray Mold

Gray mold goes by a variety of names such as ash mold or ghost spot. Regardless of the name you call it, you can spot it easily. It begins as little gray spots on your plants that start to turn into a fuzzy gray abrasion that eats away at your plant until it's entirely brown and nothing more than a disgusting mush. Gray mold can be found on a bunch of plants but it is particularly familiar to anyone that has grown strawberries as it completely ruins the berries it infects.

Gray mold likes to settle in near the bottom of the plant and in the areas that the plant shadows the most. It tends to begin on flowers that have wilted and then it quickly spreads out to the leaves and stem. It really likes those areas with a high humidity. The infected plants will begin to rot away and if left untreated, gray mold is one of the most disgusting diseases to have to deal with. The spores like cool temperatures and high humidity and they can get into the healthy tissue of the plants directly so your plants are especially susceptible after a trimming.

Pruning your plants or setting up on with a trellis helps to improve the air circulation and lower the humidity of your plants so that gray mold will desire them less. You can also use a small fan to increase the airflow around your plants. Always remove any fallen plant matter. If you spray your plants down in the morning, give them time to dry so that gray mold is less interested in the bed. Fungicides can also help in tackling gray mold infections.

Preventing Disease

We saw in the last chapter how we maintain our hydroponic gardens. These steps are also important because they help us to prevent disease from taking hold in our gardens. Because they are directly related to our conversation here in this chapter, you will recognize a lot of this information. However, it is of vital importance in keeping disease out of your garden so it is worth restating.

The most important thing we can do to help our plants avoid becoming diseased is to make sure that they are healthy and not overly stressed. This means we want to check our pH and EC levels regularly to make sure that they are in the proper range. We also want to make sure that we clean our reservoir from time to time and have a schedule for cycling out the old solution and filling it back up with a new, freshly balanced one. This will help your plants to stay healthy which helps them to fend off attacks by pathogens.

You also want to keep your garden as clean as possible. Like with pests, using a two-door airlock system will give you an area in which to wipe down and clean up before you enter into the garden. Doing this helps to remove dirt from your person, which is absolutely the leading way for pathogens to get introduced into your setup. Make sure to clean your hands and any tools you plan to use in the garden before you start messing around. Also, clean off your boots and consider removing any jacket or outdoor wear that you have on.

Clean up any spills as soon as they happen to avoid introducing extra moisture and humidity around your plants as these attract disease. Also make sure that you are removing any dead plant matter as soon as you spot it. Dead plant matter becomes a breeding ground for both pests and disease. Check your plants for disease regularly and remove any that show signs of heavy infection. Consider washing your plants down twice a week or so to knock off any pests or infection that may be trying to take hold.

By keeping vigilant and maintaining your garden, you can prevent disease from taking hold and ensure that you are raising healthy, beautiful crops.

Chapter Summary

- Pests can be one of the most annoying parts of tending a hydroponic garden but proper care will help to prevent infestation.

- Spider mites are tiny spiders that eat away at your plants and cause tiny brown and yellow spots all over the leaves.

- Spider mites can be identified by the spider-like webbing they leave behind or trails of blood left behind when you wipe the bottoms of leaves.

- You can deal with spider mites by hosing off your plants or introducing beneficial insects into your garden.

- Aphids are little lice-like pests that feed off the juices of your plants and leave them misshapen, yellowed and covered in a sticky substance known as honeydew.

- Spraying down the plants can help to dislodge aphids. A dusting of flour on your plants will constipate any aphids and help to start them migrating away from your garden. A soapy water mixture can also be used to kill them off.

- Thrips are tiny creatures that leave little metallic black specks all over the leaves of your plants.

- Thrips lay their eggs inside your plants, so hose off your plants, remove any infested plants and consider introducing beneficial insects to the garden to eat the thrips.

- Fungus gnats don't harm your garden when they are in their adult stage but their larvae snack on the roots of your plants which causes them to wilt, yellow and causes stunting of growth.

- Fungus gnat larvae take up in your growing medium, so check the plant beds for infestation. If a plant sends up a bunch of adult gnats, you can assume it to be infected and dispose of it. Spraying your plants with flying insect killer can help take care of gnats as well.

- Whiteflies look like little moths and they love sucking your plants dry, leaving them with white spots or yellowing of the leaves.

- Introduce beneficial insects to the garden to deal with whiteflies. Hosing off plants also helps and organic pesticides serve as a last-ditch effort against them.

- Always check with your local hydroponic or gardening store to see if pests in your area are immune to any of the known treatment options.

- Limiting access to your garden will help to limit the chances of infestation. Screen doors and airlocks offer great protection.

- Set up blue and yellow traps in and around your garden, making sure to have some around the stem of your plants. These give early warnings of infestation.

- Check your plants and spray them off with water from time to time. A thorough check twice a week should be enough.

- If you are planning to introduce a new plant into your garden, make sure that you quarantine it and check it thoroughly for infestation and infection before you plant it.

- Iron deficiency causes your plants to have dark green veins and yellowing of the middle. Check pH and EC levels for signs of problems. Spray liquid iron to see if it helps and consider introducing more iron into your nutrient mix.

- Powdery mildew is like a white dusting on top of your plants that can cause leaves to die off. Open the plant to better airflow, remove any infected foliage and consider a milk-water spray as well as washing the plants from time to time.

- Gray mold is the grossest of the diseases and the easiest to spot. Prune plants to open them up to better airflow, remove dead plant matter or infected matter and consider using a fungicide.

- Preventing disease is best done by keeping our plants nice and healthy. If you follow the steps outlined in chapter 5, check your plants for signs of infection and take care of them with scheduled washes then you should be able to prevent major harm from coming to your garden.

In the next chapter, we will look at some of the mistakes that new growers are prone to make and see how we can avoid making them ourselves. We'll also look at some of the myths surrounding hydroponic growing to dispel any false ideas we may still have about it.

CHAPTER SEVEN

MYTHS AND MISTAKES TO AVOID

Our time together has almost come to a close. Before you go out and get going on your own garden, let us take the time to look at some of the mistakes and myths that pop up frequently in discussions on hydroponic gardening. By digging through the myths to find the truth and learning from the mistakes of those that came before us, we are able to benefit from the knowledge and avoid making the same mistakes ourselves.

Mistake: Hard-to-Use Setups

When you are setting up your hydroponic garden, it is important that you consider how hard it will be to use. Are you going to have a difficult time reaching the plants in the back because you put the garden up against a wall? Are you going to bump into the lights every time you try to tend the bed because the space is too small and cramped?

When you are setting up your garden it is important that you consider issues such as the physical space in which it will sit. You want to make sure that you can get to all your plants without a struggle. If you're knocking over lights or throwing your back out to reach plants then the setup isn't going to be a very good one. Chances are you are going to end up breaking something or neglecting it. Consider the ways in which you move through the garden space; make sure that you are able to reach everything.

You also want to make sure that you are able to get to your reservoir easily. While it may be tempting just to rest the grow tray on top of the reservoir, consider how this might cause issues when it comes time to switch the nutrient solution. Will you have somewhere to place the grow tray while you have to mess around with the reservoir? If not, then how did you plan to do it?

We saw in chapter five all the different steps we take to maintain our hydroponic garden. Read those steps again before you set up your garden and make sure that your setup allows you to actually get in the garden and take those actions. If not, then you will want to reconsider your design.

Myth: Hydroponic Gardens Are Only for Illegal Substances

It seems that any time hydroponics pop up in the news it is in relation to some illegal grow operation that has been busted by the police. This has led to a stigma around hydroponics, one which it really doesn't deserve. Just because it happens that a lot of illegal growers use hydroponic setups, it doesn't mean that hydroponics is used just for illegal purposes.

As we saw above, we went an entire book looking at hydroponics and never once did we mention any drugs. We looked at how hydroponics will help our herb gardens to produce 30% more aromatic oils. We talked about vegetables and fruits. Never once did we speak about illegal substances.

This is because hydroponics is a system for growing plants. Those plants don't need to be illegal. They can be, yes. But they can also be the garden veggies you serve in a salad. Hydroponics is just a great system for growing plants and it is a system that you can run from inside your house, which means that you can hide your garden easily. But hydroponics itself is not illegal, it does not mean that you are taking part in illegal activities and this particular myth should be put to rest already.

Mistake: Choosing the Wrong Crops for Your Climate

You hear about a new crop on one of the gardening sites you check online. It sounds like it could be a lot of fun to grow, some kind of berry you never heard of before and people say it does great in a hydroponic setup. You order some seeds, plant it and it grows but it just doesn't give the results you wanted. Looking to see what goes wrong, you do some more Googling on the plant and you realize it needs to be in a super-hot, arid environment. And you're living through the coldest winter of your life.

Different plants want different climates and nothing will be more disappointing than trying to grow a plant that just doesn't like the climate you can offer. We should always do our research on the plants that we want to grow. We can do this easily with Google or by going into our local hydroponic store to speak to the staff.

Myth: Hydroponics Have to be Done Indoors

We've spoken a lot about indoor hydroponics in this book. This was a choice to highlight the fact that we can raise hydroponics indoors. There any many people out there who don't have access to an outside plot in which to start a garden. Most people that live in an apartment building have at best a balcony and many don't even have that much. Being that you can have an indoor garden, hydroponics offers a way for more people to get into gardening.

But this doesn't mean that you can't have an outdoor hydroponic garden. When we raise our gardens indoors, we are able to control the seasons and really take an active role in maintaining the humidity and temperature, how long the grow lights are on and much more. If we grow outdoors then we can save money on grow lights by using the sun but we also open our garden up to more risk from pests and disease. However, hydroponics can be done anywhere that you want.

Mistake: Picking the Wrong Plants for Your Setup

This could also be called "Not Doing Your Research." Like picking plants that match your climate, you are also going to want to make sure you pick plants that will work well in your setup. Some plants work better in different systems. Some want less water; some want slower draining and others want more water and others yet want faster draining.

It is important that you research the plants that you want to put in your garden. There are hundreds upon hundreds of websites jam-packed with information about every plant you could consider growing. They will tell you the pH and EC levels for the plant, how hot they like their environment, how much water they want and what type of hydroponic setup is best for them. We looked at a handful throughout this book but there is no way we could have covered all of them. But Google is your friend.

So make sure you do your research and plan out your garden. Preparing yourself with information will avoid costly mistakes. Not only does it cost to grow but there is also a time cost and you will lose weeks before you realize that growing that one plant is a losing battle.

Myth: Hydroponics is Super Expensive

This myth has good reason to be around. The truth is that hydroponics can be expensive. Can be. But just because it can be doesn't mean that it always is. When you head to the hydroponic store and look at all the prices and get talked into buying more than you really needed, then it is going to be expensive. But like many hobbies, it depends on how serious you want to take it and you can always start slow.

There are a ton of ways to cut down costs when beginning your garden. Searching online you can find hundreds of do-it-yourself guides to starting a hydroponic setup. We looked at three pretty cheap options ourselves in chapter two. These offer great ways to try out hydroponic gardening for the new grower. You can get your hands dirty and really see if it is something that you enjoy before you go spending a lot of money. Speaking of spending a lot of money...

Mistake: Scaling Up the Operation Too Early

Starting off too big can be a terrible mistake. For one, it means sinking a lot of money into growing right out the gate. Before you do this you should at least have some experience with hydroponics. Another big issue is that until you have some experience you don't actually know how to best care for your garden and every step in the operation cycle is going to be a learning experience. This isn't bad when we start small but starting bigger means any mistakes we make along the way are going to cost us that much more.

You should start slow and learn the ropes. As you go along you can buy more expensive equipment as you figure out what equipment you actually need and what equipment works best with your style of growing. As you learn the way your plants take to the system, get a feel for how they grow in your setup, then you can begin to expand. You can start to add in another grow tray, maybe two. But add slowly, take your time and make sure you have a good grasp of how to run a small garden before you jump into a large one. You can always get there but patience will help save you from some truly devastating mistakes along the way. It's one thing to mess up one grow tray, it's another to mess up a dozen.

Myth: Hydroponics is Unnatural

What happened to just sticking a plant in the ground and letting it grow? Hydroponics seems like a lot of work to do the same thing. The plants come out bigger, too. Seems like there must be something unnatural going on here. It must be all those chemicals used in the solution.

Of course, this myth is just silly. We are growing plants and using natural mix in our grow trays. We mix together a nutrient solution but all of these are natural nutrients that the plants take from the Earth anyway. Hydroponics is just a system of growing. We grow healthy plants the same as any gardener tries to. There are no gross chemicals being used to give us better growth than soil. All we are doing is using the natural desires of the plant to provide it with the most comfortable growing experience we can.

In a way, hydroponics is almost like owning a pet. There are wild dogs in the world but nobody thinks it is unhealthy to have a pet dog. We are treating our plants the same; we are providing for their needs so that they can focus on living. Just in

147

the case of plants, living means growing into fruit or vegetables that we can enjoy afterward!

Mistake: Not Maintaining Your Garden

I know, I know. You've heard this one before. But it is the number one mistake that new growers make and so we are going to speak about it one last time. The fact is that maintaining your garden doesn't just mean changing the water. It doesn't just mean we look at the garden when the plants look ill and infected and get to work. Maintaining our gardens is a commitment that any gardener has to honor.

Something spill? Better wipe that up. There's dead plant matter in your grow tray or on the floor around your setup? Best clean that up and get rid of it. Infestations and infections love to grow in these conditions. So, check your plants, test the water, clean up the beds and show them a little love. You wouldn't let your dog sleep in its own waste, so why would you let your plants? Maintaining your garden is the most important thing you can do as a new grower.

Treat your plants right.

Mistake: Forgetting to Have Fun

If you are growing because you want to sell your crops, that's a fine reason to do it. But try to have fun. For many, this is an enjoyable hobby and brings them a lot of peace. When you start to get money involved, it can be easy to lose track of that. Don't forget to take time to smell the roses. Or the tomatoes, whatever it is you're growing.

Chapter Summary

- You want to design your hydroponic garden so that it is easy to get at all of your plants and access the reservoir without bumping into things or knocking over your lights.

- While many people who grow illegal crops use hydroponic gardens, there is nothing illegal about the systems of hydroponics nor does it need to be used for illegal means.

- Make sure you find out if the plants you want to grow will work for your climate.

- Indoor gardens offer us more control of our hydroponic environment but this does not mean that you have to put your hydroponic garden inside.

- Always do your research on the plants you want to grow. Make sure that they work in your setup, environment, and at your pH/EC levels.

- Hydroponics can be an expensive hobby but it doesn't cost a lot of money to get started and there are many DIY guides available to help you get into growing.

- Start small and work your way up to a large garden so that you know how to best take care of your plants.
- There is nothing unnatural about hydroponic gardening.
- Remove dead plant matter, clean up spills, check the pH and EC levels. Not maintaining your garden is a sure-fire way to lose it and the biggest mistake new growers make.
- Have fun out there!

FINAL WORDS

We've come a long way throughout the course of this book. Starting with a definition of hydroponics, we're covered a lot of information that will help you to get started on your own hydroponic garden. Before we close, let's go over a brief summary of what we covered and share some words on where to go from here.

Hydroponics has been around for literally ages but it is only just starting to pick up some serious interest. These gardens can take a bit of work to set up and maintain but they offer a great way of growing crops. We focused here on those looking to get started with hydroponics, so we tailored our information towards the beginner. The lessons we covered, however, have everything the beginner needs to get started and begin the road to expert.

We have six primary setups to choose from when it comes to what kind of system we want to set up. We saw how to set up deep water, wicking and drip systems. These are the easiest systems for DIY setups and beginners but there are also aeroponics, ebb and flow and nutrient film technique systems. These systems are more complicated than is recommended for a beginner but I encourage you to research these more as you get more comfortable with hydroponics.

There are four key elements that we looked at as the operation cycle of the hydroponic garden. These are soiling, seeding, lighting and trimming. By understanding how each of these elements works, we are able to handle the growing cycle of our plants. There are many options available for soiling and several for lighting. Finding the combination that is right for you will take some research but it should ultimately be decided on what plants you want to grow.

Speaking of plants, we have seen that there are a ton of plants that work really well in hydroponic gardens. Herbs grown in a hydroponic garden have 30% more aromatic oils than those grown in soil. Lettuce in particular absolutely adores growing hydroponically. Each plant has its own preferences when it comes to how much water it wants, the pH level it likes best and the temperature that it needs to grow. For this reason, we have to research our plants and make sure that we only grow those that are compatible together.

We also learned how to mix our own nutrient solutions so that we can provide our plants with what they need to grow. There are a lot of pre-mixed options available for purchase as well. Taking control of our own mix is just another way we are able to get closer to our plants and provide for them to the best of our ability.

The importance of maintaining a clean garden cannot be stressed enough and so we spent time learning how we care for our gardens. The information in chapter five can be used to build your own maintenance schedule. To do this, look at how often each step of maintenance needs to be performed and plan ahead so that you don't forget. It's super important that we take care of our plants because we don't want them in dirty environments nor do we want them to be overly stressed. A dirty environment and a stressed plant are a recipe for infestation and infection.

We explored some of the most common pests that attack our plants. However, we didn't cover all of them. That would take a whole book. The pests we covered are the most likely ones you will have to deal with but that doesn't mean they will be the only ones. It is a good thing we also learned how to prevent pests. The preventive steps we learned will also help us to spot any pests we did not cover. If you find something you don't recognize in one of your traps then you know it's time for more research. Remember too that not every insect is a pest, some help us out by eating pests!

Infection is a risk with all gardens and so our number one tool in preventing harmful pathogens from attacking our plants is to make sure that our plants are nice and strong. We clean our gardens, we provide them with nutrients mixed to their liking, we give them the love and care they need and in doing this we keep them healthy and unstressed. While infection can still take hold in a healthy plant, it is far more likely to attack stressed plants. This preventative step combines what we learned in chapter six about pests and infection with the skills we practice in chapter five.

Finally, we looked at mistakes that are common to beginning hydroponic gardeners. We also exploded those myths that surround hydroponics to dispel the lies and untruths surrounding our newfound hobby. Searching online for tips or mistakes will reveal many discussions with hydroponic gardeners that are written specifically to help beginners like you to have the easiest, most enjoyable time possible getting into this form of gardening.

If you're excited to get started then I suggest you begin planning out your garden now. You will need to dedicate a space for it and pick which system is most appealing to you and your skill level. Write down the plants you are most interested in growing and begin gathering information about them; what environment do they like best? What temperature? How much light do they need? What pH level?

Once you know what plants you want to grow and what system you want, you can start to build a shopping list. Along with the hardware to set up the system itself, don't forget to get some pH testing kits and an EC meter. Also make sure you have cleaning material, as you know now how important it is to sanitize and sterilize your equipment. This is also a great time to build your maintenance schedule.

Once you have this information you can return to this book and use it as a manual for walking through every step of the growing process. The information that we covered will take you from beginner and, along with the application of practice, turn you into a pro in no time. But most importantly, don't forget to have fun!

Lightning Source UK Ltd.
Milton Keynes UK
UKHW021834230220
359192UK00013B/372

9 781951 345020